1,000,000 Books

are available to read at

Forgotten Books

www.ForgottenBooks.com

Read online
Download PDF
Purchase in print

ISBN 978-1-330-80521-3
PIBN 10107700

This book is a reproduction of an important historical work. Forgotten Books uses state-of-the-art technology to digitally reconstruct the work, preserving the original format whilst repairing imperfections present in the aged copy. In rare cases, an imperfection in the original, such as a blemish or missing page, may be replicated in our edition. We do, however, repair the vast majority of imperfections successfully; any imperfections that remain are intentionally left to preserve the state of such historical works.

Forgotten Books is a registered trademark of FB &c Ltd.
Copyright © 2018 FB &c Ltd.
FB &c Ltd, Dalton House, 60 Windsor Avenue, London, SW19 2RR.
Company number 08720141. Registered in England and Wales.

For support please visit www.forgottenbooks.com

1 MONTH OF FREE READING

at

www.ForgottenBooks.com

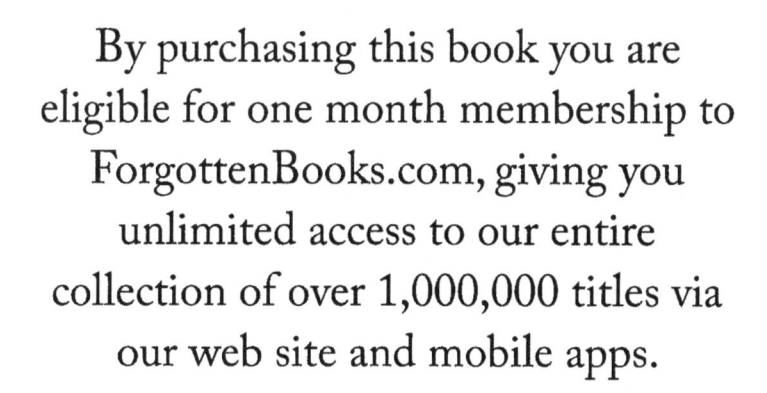

By purchasing this book you are eligible for one month membership to ForgottenBooks.com, giving you unlimited access to our entire collection of over 1,000,000 titles via our web site and mobile apps.

To claim your free month visit: www.forgottenbooks.com/free107700

* Offer is valid for 45 days from date of purchase. Terms and conditions apply.

English
Français
Deutsche
Italiano
Español
Português

www.forgottenbooks.com

Mythology Photography **Fiction**
Fishing Christianity **Art** Cooking
Essays Buddhism Freemasonry
Medicine **Biology** Music **Ancient Egypt** Evolution Carpentry Physics
Dance Geology **Mathematics** Fitness
Shakespeare **Folklore** Yoga Marketing
Confidence Immortality Biographies
Poetry **Psychology** Witchcraft
Electronics Chemistry History **Law**
Accounting **Philosophy** Anthropology
Alchemy Drama Quantum Mechanics
Atheism Sexual Health **Ancient History**
Entrepreneurship Languages Sport
Paleontology Needlework Islam
Metaphysics Investment Archaeology
Parenting Statistics Criminology
Motivational

DUBLIN TO HAVE A CITY MANAGER.
[Detroit News.]

Dublin, capital of the Irish Free State, is going to try a new variation of the city manager plan, if the bill goes through parliament unamended. Instead of being appointed by the council, the city manager will be named by a civil service commission. To remove him it will take a two-thirds vote of the council, plus the acquiescence of one of the members of the national cabinet. The latter provision is probably included because the government owns much property in Dublin and thus has a vital interest in the manner in which the city is run by the manager.

There is some criticism reported from citizens because the bill does not closely define the relations between the city manager and the council, about the only real check on the city manager being the council's control of the budget. But that check is the most important of all, and Dublin is likely to discover that the manager will not be likely to try to override the council while it holds the pursestrings and can keep him from realizing some of his cherished objects.

It has been the experience of American cities that have adopted the city manager plan that a city manager who keeps his head and who adopts wise policies will have the general public behind him, and since the jobs of the council members depend on the public, they are not likely to become too vigorous in opposition to his plans. If, on the other hand, the manager defies public opinion, a council is likely to be elected that will deprive him of his position.

*eland's dead and gone,
O'Leary in the grave.*

. Compulsory Irish as-
:nsorship of literature has
 service, and only the poets
rn. There is no place for
the Free State mind which
of a hard technical school
gions sentiment, and public
,r, mind you, they are out
streets, municipal adminis-
:ature. All day the landed
itry read the safe columns
es in the still safer precincts
street Club. What will we
hooley? Drum him out of
! Bad form! Dirt! Evil
 country's going from bad
the bishop said the nightin-
nmoral bird. Yes, said the
iblic Morals, any nightin-
nto this country will be
t. *Everything* is most im-
Shaw, Shakespeare, and the

d "the North side" lingers
entury. Forgotten Dublin.
:r! Farwell to the Rakes of
 ore's melodies and Daly's
 arewell to Fanny This and
 Their white muslin gowns
 iseum pieces. Their harps
'.
:y of Leopold Bloom. This
[r. Gilhooley. This is the
 sh Free State.
 :o Mr. Lennox Robinson,
witty, lectured to that select
 Literary Society. The sub-
:e was "The Younger Irish
 proceeded to intimidate us
ly that there were eleven
 s, all very much alive and
able poetry. *Eleven* young

Possibly three out of the eleven will writ
poetry when they have reached years of dis
cretion. Fifty is, I believe, years of dis
cretion. On the other hand, I do not be
lieve that discretion is the better part o
poetry. Consider Keats, consider Shelley
Byron, Rimbaud, any poet that ever wa
has written his best before thirty. I hav
neither time nor space to give the names o
the eleven, but I am sure of the followin
three—and they have all a few years befor
thirty—Lyle Donaghy, Geoffrey Phibb
(now known as Geoffrey Taylor), an
Frank O'Connor. Lyle Donaghy, th
youngest, is in London under the shelterin
wing of T. S. Eliot. Frank O'Connor—
Cork man—is at present working in Dub
lin, and Geoffrey Taylor, between the inter
vals of making history for the Lytto
Strachey of 1980, is working in England.

Ireland's national theatre has just con
cluded a rather sterile year, and 1930 s
far is unproductive of fresh genius. N
new O'Casey has arisen from the slums. N
young Synge has come out of the West
There is a dearth of fresh talent in actor
as well as dramatics. Barry FitzGerald
the well-beloved, the King of Comedians
has left us for London, and there is no on
to take his place. Yet I feel it is only th
calm that comes before a storm. Genius i
brewing somewhere, and it is only a ques
tion of time before it appears.

Lennox Robinson, on his return from
lecture tour in the States, wrote a pla
called "Ever the Twain," which was pro
duced at the Abbey Theatre last autum
and revived a few weeks ago. It is ru
mored that J. B. Fagan intends to produc
it in London and eventually take it to Ne
York. The play is written round the ex
periences of a group of lecturers and thei
various reactions to American life and man
ners. Padraic Colum says that everyone a
the first presentation had either lectured i
America or wanted to lecture there. Cer

He just gets there and something always happens to mar the effect. He started off with that grim novel, "The Valley of the Squinting Windows," which ran into several editions in England and America and evoked public demonstrations and legal actions on its first appearance. Then he wrote two of the funniest and most lighthearted comedies in the Abbey Theatre repertoire, which he followed up by a powerful, depressing and at times very dull play, "The Master." At present he is engaged on a new play, "A Grand House in the City," which is about Dublin life, and he has just finished a novel, "Return to Ebontheever" a story of Westmeath thirty-five years ago. Brinsley MacNamara is experimenting and when he has found himself he will write excellent plays. He is as much a contradiction in himself as he is in his work. He looks like a jolly, hearty, blue-eyed, black-haired farmer, and he is really the most moody, aloof, and unsociable of Dubliners. He rarely appears except at an Abbey first night.

Those two voluntary exiles, Sean O'Casey and Liam O'Flaherty, are both living in London. The Abbey directors have maintained a sinister calm over "The Silver Tassie." They have remained silent even when the London critics foamed over the London production of this amazing play and compared O'Casey very favorably to Shakespeare. I saw "The Silver Tassie" and thought it was a curiously uneven production. At times it was greater than anything O'Casey had ever done, and there were moments when I hoped he would never sink so low again—the telephone episode for instance. The acting was bad, except for Barry FitzGerald, and the production was inaccurate and stupid except in the extraordinary second act. O'Casey has only produced one play since he went to London, and "Juno" still remains his masterpiece.

As for O'Flaherty, he still continues to write his powerful studies of brutes in

DUBLIN
EXPLORATIONS
AND REFLECTIONS
BY AN ENGLISHMAN

MAUNSEL & CO., LTD.
DUBLIN: 50 LOWER BAGGOT ST.
LONDON: 40 MUSEUM STREET
1917

PRINTED BY JOHN FALCONER, DUBLIN.

CONTENTS

CHAP		PAGE
I.	From Euston to North Wall	1
II.	First Impressions of the Natives	22
III.	The North Side	41
IV.	South Dublin	63
V.	Hills and the Sea	84
VI.	The Municipal Gallery of Modern Art	101
VII.	The National Portrait Gallery	125
VIII.	The National Gallery of Ireland	145
IX.	The Intellectuals	165
X.	Literature in Dublin	192
XI.	The Theatre in Dublin	240
XII.	Farewell	258

TO

B. D.

DUBLIN
EXPLORATIONS AND REFLECTIONS

CHAPTER I.

From Euston to North Wall.

Of all the London termini, I think Euston is architecturally the most exciting. There is something almost Egyptian in the hugeness of its entrance gates, in the vast spaces of its central hall. On the warm June evening when I drove up to its portals—*en route* for the capital of an island remote and glamourous—its air of mystery was more noticeable than ever.

Once inside the station, however, the familiar thrill of " going abroad " overcame all others. I am of those who feel asphyxiated if they are unable, for at least once in every year, to take a lonely plunge into some foreign country. The war among its minor horrors seemed to have made foreign travel impossible for a non-combatant, until, amid the tragedy of Easter week, had come the realisation that Ireland was a foreign country, that the St. George's Channel was broader than the Pas de Calais, and that to almost every Englishman, myself included, the land of the Gael was utterly unknown.

It was, I feel sure, with all the emotions of the explorer that I took my ticket for Dublin, pleased to be going to such a savage spot without a revolver and armed only with sympathy and a curiosity which grew to fever pitch as the train hurried northwards and westwards through the sleeping countryside. The train was filled almost entirely with soldiers; there could not have been more than a dozen civilians on board. The men in my compartment, after going through the soldier's charming ritual of making friends—handing Woodbines to one another, exchanging " comics," and so on—soon began the inevitable discussion about scandals which seems to start whenever soldiers get together. They all gave their opinions as to what should be done when the war was over. To judge from their tone, the flight of the entire Cabinet to America on the Day of Reckoning would (from the Cabinet's point of view) be an advisable course. "If you ask me," said the sergeant, " it'll be a sove kee poo for 'Squith and 'is lot—the 'ole bloody gang of 'em." Only one of the soldiers in my compartment was an Irishman. He had been seen off at Euston by a girl with the softest, gentlest brogue that

I have ever heard, and had amused us all by telling the girl to be sure to go regularly to the night classes, and to improve her spelling. The way they bantered one another was the prettiest thing to hear, very different from the heavy glances, the glum Cockney clichés of a London man's farewells.

Although we were all of us bound for Dublin, none of my companions ever said a word about Ireland or referred in any way to his destination. Long after they were peacefully asleep, I sat up uncomfortably in my corner, thinking about the island for which I was bound, trying to imagine what it would be like, and going over in my mind everything that I had ever heard about it. I discovered that I had really heard extraordinarily little. In my extreme youth, child of " High Church" Church people of Tory views and great readers of the *Standard* newspaper, I remembered that my parents used to discuss Mr. Gladstone's alleged iniquities. G.O.M. repeated backwards gave you M.O.G.—Murderer of Gordon! This fearful crime committed by the Grand Old Man for some reason or other became inseparably linked up in my infant mind with another, equally infamous, called " Home Rule." Mr. Gladstone had, it appeared, been guilty of both offences, and, so far as I could gather, my parents considered " Home Rule " the graver of the two.

If the Irish were given Home Rule I was led to believe that they would forthwith exterminate one another in internecine conflict. Not content with murdering Gordon, therefore, Mr. Gladstone, that very wicked man, proposed to destroy the Irish race by giving them Home Rule. But Great Britain (that is to say the Tory Party), like a benevolent auntie, was not going to allow the naughty Irish children to misbehave themselves. She was going to act *in their best interests;* she was going to deprive them of just the things they happened to want, for their own good. Every child, of course, knows what that means. Up to the age of twelve one divides aunts into " decent " aunts, and those who act " in one's best interests " by forbidding a visit to the pantomime—or whatever it is on which one happens to have set one's heart. Even in those early days I think I realised, dimly, that my father's sole reason for disapproving of Home Rule lay in the fact that it had been advocated by Mr. Gladstone. Ireland didn't really exist for him at all; only hatred of the Radicals existed.

I heard nothing more about Ireland until I went to school and made friends with an Irish boy who invested the country for me with a certain romance. His family lived in a tumble-down castle in Co. Westmeath, and he used to tell me exciting stories of his hunting exploits in the Christmas holidays, stories which blended pleasantly with the works of such widely-separated novelists as Charles Lever and Mrs. B. M. Croker. Some years after this, when schooldays were over, a new and quite different Ireland dawned on me when a friend, now dead, who was himself a poet, gave me a copy of "The Wind among the Reeds." Here was an Ireland of undreamed-of beauty, full of strange legends, of mists and twilight and sudden wild illuminations. But it was strangely unactual, this Celtic fairyland conjured up by Mr. Yeats' poetry, and I don't think it ever occurred to me that it really had anything to do with that odd-shaped Western island on the map. For the Ireland of the political geography I suppose I still entertained a vague inherited prejudice. And I was so busy examining, criticising, rejecting other more important inherited prejudices that I had no time to examine this one. Politics I hated with an intolerant loathing, and during the years when Mr. Yeats' poetry, the novels of George Moore, the plays of Synge and of Bernard Shaw were my daily mental food, the living Ireland from which these writers sprang seemed always to be wrapped in a malodorous political fog, from which the sensitive nose averted itself. I read no Irish history: that subject is avoided in English schools and universities.

I did, certainly, meet some earnest young men at Oxford who talked about " trying to find work under Sir Horace Plunkett;" but their earnestness seemed very tedious. I connected it in my mind with the earnestness of other contemporaries who proposed to go in for " social work in the East End " under the aegis of the Bishop of London. My view in those days, since I have always been a natural heretic, was that nothing required " working amongst" more vigorously than Oxford itself and that the sooner the East End—or for that matter benighted Ireland—established a mission in St. Giles' the better. From 1907, when I came to live in London, until the outbreak of the war, Ireland as a country and apart from the literature which Irishmen produced, existed for me no more than for the majority of my fellow-countrymen. " Going abroad " for me meant going to France, to Italy, to Spain, Greece or Portugal; and the only Nationalist movement with which I ever actually came in contact was that of the Jugo-Slavs in Dalmatia. Of Irish Nationalism, execpt in so far as it was represented by a proverbially tiresome group in the English House of Commons, I knew nothing and cared less. The aspirations of the Jugo-Slavs, however, became an obsession, and when I listened to the whispered confideuces of an unshaven sea captain in a café at Zara—a group of Austrian officers in high black képis and handsome light blue uniforms eyeing us sardonically meanwhile from a distant table—the temptation to imitate Byron was for the moment almost irresistible! We repaired, I remember to a kind of dark cave in a side street where a monstrous woman with one tooth in her head and clothed in evil-smelling rags, squatted underneath a huge wine barrel. Here by the light of two guttering candles standing in their own wax, the sea captain, myself, and the other conspirators sat on wooden forms and drank damnation to oppressors. Some of this enthusiasm, I must admit, evaporated as I went further down the coast seeing everywhere signs of prosperity and of the admirable government of the Austrians—good roads, good schools, and indeed every outward indication of honest and efficient rule. The grievances of the Jugo-Slavs were, it appeared, largely sentimental. But, at the same time, it was impossible not to realise the depth and genuineness of their national spirit, while the story of how it had been kept alive by the revival of their national literature and the teaching and preservation of their language under great difficulties, was one to fire the imagination. I returned to England full of those generous and sentimental enthusiasms for " smaller nations " to which—strange as it may appear to a certain section of the Irish public—the ordinary Englishman is singularly prone. I am sure it never occurred to me, while I was writing impassioned articles for Liberal newspapers about the Nationalist aspirations of the Jugo-Slavs in distant Dalmatia, that a movement of precisely the same kind could conceivably exist in "contagious" Ireland. Ireland for the average Englishman is just a part of "the British Isles": and in that phrase lies, I think, the secret of his whole attitude towards Irish politics. He will not take the trouble to use his imagination; he forgets the separating seas; the events of the past do not trouble him, for he knows and cares nothing about them. They are not his business. The admission may seem naïf, nevertheless I must confess that, until Easter week, I never actually realised that there were peoples on the earth who looked on my country as the hated tyrant! I had read Mr. Kipling's works at school; I knew all about the "white man's burden "—but I had never read a line of Lecky's "History of Ireland in the Eighteenth Century."

Two years after my visit to Dalmatia came the outbreak of the European War which had been so confidently predicted by my friends at Zara. The war has done a great deal more than upheave and batter large tracts of Europe: it has upheaved and battered the mind of every European. All our old crockery of unchallenged, inherited beliefs has been smashed to smithereens. In the gigantic crash of the war every opinion held by men on every subject has been abruptly challenged. Every sentient being capable of ratiocination has been forced to throw over long-cherished convictions and to arrive at new ones. And in consequence of this, as the war has dragged on, in all men's minds—soldiers, artisans, pacificists, no matter whom—there has grown up an intense, a passionate longing for the Truth. We are all seekers after Truth now. We can no longer accept anything at its face value; we can no longer comfortably believe anything we see in any newspaper, least of all an English newspaper; we can no longer accept anything that our fathers told us without testing it afresh for ourselves. Amid the ever thickening, ever darkening cloud of lies which composes the poisonous "fog of war," one thing only emerges like a rock to which we are safe in clinging—it is the old truth, which we might have learnt from Socrates, that we know nothing.

As I sat back in my corner in the darkened railway carriage, listening enviously to the snores of my fellow-travellers, my thoughts wandered off to the events of Easter week, which had really started me on my journey. On the evening after the first news of the Rebellion was published in London I was in a music-hall in the Edgware Road, listening to some well-meaning foreigners who were treating this district of West London to a " refined musical scena." The male performers, of whom there were four, wore evening clothes of grey silk, with knee breeches. One of them, the youngest, played the 'cello, a second the fiddle, a third played accompaniments at the piano, and the fourth—a fat, bald-headed individual who sweated profusely —delivered popular ballads in a throaty baritone. The climax of the " scena" was intended to be that most popular of London songs, " When Irish eyes are smiling." There is, I think, nothing which an Engglish music-hall audience takes so ecstatically to heart as a sentimental ballad about Ireland. (The history books will never let the world forget that it was with a song about Tipperary on their lips that our heroic little force took the field in August, 1914.) Any reference in a Yiddish brogue to " the little bit of Heaven " sprinkled with star-dust and so on, brings tears to our eyes. It has been the same as long as I can remember. In a London suburban drawing-room there are no favourites on a Sunday evening like " We're off to Philadelphia in the morning," no pathos is enjoyed more hugely than " They're hanging men and women for the wearin' o' the green."

If you were to ask any of the emotional performers whether they had any idea as to what it was all about, who hanged who and why, they would probably stare at you in amazement. If you explained, they would go on singing it just the same, with Anglo-Saxon imperviousness to " nonsense."

The performers of the "refined musical scena" at the Edgware Road music-hall understood their business perfectly, when they chose for the grand finale which was to bring them innumerable recalls such a song as " When Irish eyes are smiling." Unluckily for them, however, the Rebellion provided a totally unexpected complication. The news had just come through, popular indignation against Ireland ran high, and no one knew how much of the truth had got into the papers. There was a widespread belief that Ireland was full of Germans who, after massacring all the English soldiers in Dublin and the rest of Ireland, would proceed to swoop down on London. It was a difficult situation for the poor " artistes." Evidently the singer had not another song which he could substitute at a moment's notice. (He looked like an Austrian Jew, and probably had but little English.) He succeeded, however, in solving the problem to his own satisfaction, and that night the audience listened to the strains of "Where *British* eyes are smiling," with feelings of puzzled confusion.

When the first news of the Rebellion came to England, it seemed to me as no doubt it seemed to the vast majority of my fellow-countrymen, rather low-down of the Irish to seize the moment of our embarrassment to stab us in the back. But for some reason which I am quite unable to explain, that ridiculous episode in the music-hall seemed to utter a warning against hasty judgment. There must be a great deal more in it than met the eye. People don't rebel for no reason at all. However addicted to practical jokes the Sinn Feiners might be, they would hardly have gone so far as to sacrifice their lives simply to a perverted sense of humour. Weeks after, when the Rebellion had been stamped out and the leaders executed, sure enough a few revealing details began to trickle through which corrected many of the ideas conceived by most of us during what was (to put it frankly) a time of anxiety. In retrospect the Dublin revolt appeared already as easily the most dramatic episode in a war which in some respects has been one of the dullest in history. And it was soon evident that never before had England displayed her genius for putting herself in an odious light more unfortunately than in the way in which she suppressed it. It was not the soldiers who were at fault. So far as one could tell (and all that I afterwards heard confirmed this impression) they behaved admirably on the whole, considering that the forces engaged were largely unseasoned troops, and that the operations were of a particularly difficult and trying nature. Such "atrocities" as have been alleged against them—such as the North King Street shootings—were probably due to fright and overstrained nerves. The murder of Mr. Sheehy-Skeffington and his companions was a sheer stroke of ill-fortune for England for which it is difficult to see how she can justly be abused. The actual culprit, moreover, was an Irishman. But having suffered the disaster of this ghastly deed one would have thought those responsible for general questions of policy would have paused and taken thought. Not so. The methods employed in suppressing the Rebellion of 1916 were precisely similar to the methods employed in suppressing the Rebellions of 1798 and 1803. The military mind had apparently remained impervious to new ideas throughout the intervening century. In spite of all the harm done in the past to Anglo-Irish relations by the making of martyrs and national heroes, more martyrs and more national heroes were made, and the prestige of England was permanently lowered in the eyes of America and of the neutral world. She has never since been able to regain the position then lost. If the murder of Mr. Sheehy-

Skeffington was simply a piece of bad luck for England, for the attempts made to hush-up that tragic business she had no one but herself to blame.

These attempts were not successful, they were persisted in for a week or two, then dropped, under pressure, in such a manner as gravely to shake public confidence in the administration. There was something bungling and ignoble in the whole proceeding. England behaved like a good-hearted, respectable rich man put in a false and ignominious position by a momentary lack of moral courage. When the moment was passed the amends were adequate and dignified, but they came too late. What a contrast to all this seemed the behaviour of the rebel leaders! They were foolish, insane as it appears to us, but insanely honest and sincere. Nothing ignoble or mean or (according to their lights) ungenerous, has ever been proved against them. The inevitable reaction in England in their favour when the truth gradually emerged was very strong, and its influence is still felt. The whole episode of the Rebellion has indeed struck through the black fog of politics which formerly interposed itself between our eyes and Ireland, and in an unforgettable lightning flash has shown us Ireland's bleeding heart and our own the sword transfixing it. And it did more, that terrible revealing lightning—it showed us ourselves as we never thought to see ourselves. It is an awkward moment for a nation which has been publicly thanking God that it is not as other nations are, that it is no tyrant but the protector of the oppressed, no wicked Prussian militarist but the enemy of militarism, when it suddenly becomes suspect of the very crimes which it has set out with a flourish of trumpets to punish other races for committing. At the outbreak of the revolt we held all the cards, the sympathy was all with us. But not even the Germans could have played a hand more clumsily. After two years of war even the man in the street was capable of reflecting that there must be "something behind" the outbreak. And from this it was but a step to speculating as to what that something could be. In a little while, the alarming news came through that the executed rebels were not mere thieves and murderers in the pay of Germany, but schoolmasters and poets of blameless private lives, idealists, abstemious, self-denying men, deeply religious. What was the cause which inspired them? Who was oppressing these people? Had Ireland then really a grievance, and, if so, what was it? It was in Easter week that I asked myself this question for the first time; and I remembered the Home Rule Bill and the half-forgotten

Ulster altercation which had made the newspapers tedious in the months before the war. After the rising had been crushed my country presented herself to my mind as a rather pompous old lady, who, whilst giving herself tremendous airs of virtue, is suddenly struck in the face by a small boy who has been stood in the corner by her for a longer time than flesh and blood will endure. The old lady's consternation is pitiable. She may be pompous and absurd, however, but at least she knows how to spank. Presently, she spanks so hard, so mercilessly, that all the onlookers, and even some of the members of her own family, cry out "for shame!" But she takes no heed of them.

Whatever the Easter Rebellion may or may not have done for Ireland, I think it has helped to modify the attitude of a portion of the British public towards the war. The necessity to win through to an honourable peace has not been weakened by it; but the old confidence that we were the champions of small nations, that ours was a "Holy War," that we could never succumb to "militarism" has received a shock. Englishmen began to realise that not only were their own personal liberties for which their forefathers struggled and died being taken from them, but that their country was actually regarded as the foreign tyrant by a large proportion of the indigenous population of the sister isle. It would not surprise me if, when the war is over, the Dublin revolt were held to have done something to bring peace nearer, simply by helping to bring about the necessary " change of heart."

One effect, at least, of the Dublin Insurrection is beyond dispute. It made Ireland " actual " for the average Englishman—as actual say as Serbia or Montenegro; for a week or two, as actual as Belgium. Its Rebellion, however keenly we might resent it, had some of the crudity and brilliance of a work of youthful genius, and a marked capacity for touching the imaginations even of the unimaginative. And it had a strange quality of glamour, the glamour which attaches itself almost immediately to events which are destined to live in history. It made English people realise (for the first time in many cases) that the nation which could produce men capable of such a forlorn hope, whose unhappy circumstances urged its idealists to offer up their lives in the vain chance of bettering them, must be one of rare interest—a nation with an unconquerable soul. As for myself, I know the longing to visit Ireland first came to me, in the Edgware Road music-hall, on that evening in Easter week.

As the train bore me across Wales between lines of low hills above which gleamed the first

B

faint grey of the dawn, I felt almost as excited as I was when, as a boy, I first went alone to France. Little white houses flashed by here and there; then came a narrow arm of the sea fringed with desolate salt marshes, and finally Holyhead itself. Holyhead Station was in a tremendous bustle. A blazing electric arc-lamp shone down on it, whitening the porters' faces as they dealt with the luggage. As I went on board the steamer an individual like a steward asked me my nationality; and I noticed that the man just ahead of me answered " Irish." The rakish black steamer, comfortably appointed, seemed to compare favourably with the more familiar channel packets. The bunks looked very comfortable, and I turned in at once, glad of the chance of getting some sleep.

When I woke up, a little before eight o'clock, the coast of Ireland the mysterious was just visible under a grey sky. There was greyness everywhere; the sea was a dark slate colour. What looked like a rocky island detached itself from the mist on our right, and just ahead the tall chimney of what might have been a chemical works seemed to stand straight up out of the sea. Behind it there was a grey vista of roofs, towers, shipping. It was my first view of Dublin.

We went slowly past a small red lighthouse into the channel of the Liffey, coming to our moorings at length by a quay more grim and forbidding than anything I can remember. I left my luggage in the cloak room of the North Wall station, and walked on into the city. A drizzle of rain fell from the leaden sky, and the cobbled road was painful to one's feet. A few outside cars, heavily laden, clattered past me, the first that I had seen. The houses of grimy brick which faced the waterway seemed unutterably squalid; the forlorn pubs the dreariest of their kind. Then all at once, without warning, I found myself outside some great public building (the Custom House, as I discovered afterwards) —a fine, classical pile, carrying its size with extreme elegance and grace. Its central feature was a domed clock tower surmounted by a carved stone figure. The façade of this building looked so attractive even at close quarters that I determined to cross the river in order to see it in proper perspective. Just as I was making for the Butt Bridge, however, I caught a glimpse of the shell-battered walls of Liberty Hall, and the beginnings of "Wipers on the Liffey" becoming now apparent, everything else was for the moment forgotten. So this was modern warfare! I saw in front of me the shells of houses, with ruined walls sticking up jagged into the forlorn sky; a great stone building (the G.P.O.) with a long line of empty, staring windows;

houses all mottled and spattered with rifle fire; dust everywhere; acres of rubble and collapsed brickwork; bent iron; gaping cellars—at least half of a great thoroughfare pounded almost to pieces. And amidst all this confusion I noticed (not without a thrill) a drab, demure stone building looking rather like a disused Baptist chapel, on which were the sacred words, " The Abbey Theatre."

I think my first day in Dublin was the most crowded that I have ever spent in any foreign city, even including Paris. I raced about on tramcars; at terribly unconventional hours I presented letters of introduction; I looked about everywhere (in vain) for signs of " martial law," quite expecting bodies of soldiers to appear suddenly and execute a few well-chosen bayonet manœuvres for the benefit of their prestige. I explored Rathmines and Stephen's Green; I lunched in a café off scrambled eggs and other oddments only to find that everyone else in the place was quite content with rolls and butter. I went to Merrion Square, and then to Harcourt Street, where I spent an hour or two in the Municipal Art Gallery. Finally, in the last stages of collapse, I arrived for dinner at the house of a lady to whom I had been given an introduction, and found myself, soon afterwards, in the midst of my first Dublin " evening." My luggage had, meanwhile, been taken to an hotel on the north side to which I had been recommended; and it was in a dilapidated mansion with a splendid stone staircase and lofty rooms—evidently a good example of a Georgian town house—that I finally laid my exhausted head against the pillow, beneath a remote and dusty canopy. I fell asleep with the soft blarney of the chamber-maid echoing in my brain—she had forgotten to provide me with soap or towel, or even to give me a candle to light myself up the great stone staircase— and her execrable Dublin accent was the rarest music to my unaccustomed ears. In my dreams that night Kathleen ni Houlihan herself stooped down to fill me a crystal goblet from the Well of the Saints. And as she handed it across to me she murmured, " Sure now, I'll bring ye the soap in a minuut."

CHAPTER II.

First Impressions of the Natives.

There was no system of calling the guests in the morning at my hotel. The pressing of an electric bell in my bedroom produced loud noises away below in the deep stone caverns of the house, but no one seemed to heed them. Descending in search of a bathroom, I discovered one or two vague forms lurking in the passages, half-clad and still dreaming, perhaps, of last night's strong but shadowy waters. I tackled one of the ghosts, who answered me with the greatest politeness and led me down to the ground floor and along an interminable corridor to a kind of outhouse called "the return." A battered old barn-door cock came blinking up the stone staircase from the cellars to watch the intruders; and when the bathroom door was at last reached and dragged open there was a tremendous squawking and fluttering of wings, followed by a hasty exit of hens. The hens were much annoyed at being disturbed from their stronghold, and when I saw the bath I regretted having disarranged them. The bath was made of rusty iron, the hot tap, never

FIRST IMPRESSIONS 23

having been turned, had become securely fixed. This did not matter, for there was no hot water. Through the little window of the room the morose morning eye of the cold-bather was gladdened by a vista of ruined stables with gaping roofs and tottering walls —stables built a hundred and fifty years ago to house the chariots and horses of the Earl of Charleville. Now weeds and long grass grew up within them, and a poor bitch, banished from the house for her bad manners, howled dismally from that wilderness of decay. I could easily imagine anyone hanging himself in that bathroom!

The astonishing thing about the hotel was the fact that (except for the bathroom) it was not nearly so uncomfortable as it looked. When I succeeded in getting a hip-bath brought up to my bedroom I began positively to like it. The servants were vague but friendly, and the whole place wore an air of cheerfulness and ease.

As for the house, to a Georgian fanatic like myself, it held innumerable surprises and delights. Great canvases, so smoke-begrimed that nothing could be made of them, hung half out of their frames on the walls of one of the wide stone staircases; the beautifully designed moulding over the door of the saloon was cracked and chipped; but most of the original mahogany doors with their dropping brass handles had been preserved, and here and there a carved marble chimneypiece. With its air of decayed magnificence, the hotel suggested one of Cruikshank's illustrations to Harry Lorrequer. Oddly enough the house must have been very familiar to Charles Lever, for I found out afterwards that it had at one time been used by a clergyman as a school, and that Lever was one of his pupils.

The inhabitants of the hotel, the *pensionnaires*, had the same air of shabby-gentility as the house itself. There were only five of them, and they each had peculiarities which the wild-eyed parlour-maid made it her business to study. One of the inmates, a faded spinster well on in years, had two ruling passions— pity for the banished wire-haired terrier, which she fed surreptitiously after every meal; and anxiety to remain " select." She enjoyed talking about the finest *ariss*tocrats to a west of Ireland landowner and his wife who also lived in the house, and the question as to whether such and such a Kingstown boarding-house was or was not " select " was argued eagerly at every meal. The residents used to talk to one another in shouts, from little tables placed in different corners round the vast diningroom—and I all alone at the long table in the middle, gazing demurely at my plate. It was an odd house, the oddest I have ever been in, but it had a charm of its own—a charm difficult to analyse but impossible to resist. For one thing, everyone in the place had such good manners, even the lazy and incapable servants. The parlour-maid was fiery and temperamental, occasionally rather rude, but never insolent like an English servant. When she got into a fury (as she did at moments) and smacked one of the other servants in the eye, I found her irresistible; and I loved the way she had of roaming about the big rooms with a couple of cigarettes stuck behind her ear!

My first week in Dublin passed very happily in a more or less aimless perambulation of the streets, and in looking at the people. They seemed quite unlike any other English-speaking people with whom I had ever come in contact. They had often the strangest faces! And they appeared altogether lacking in outward uniformity, tending to go to extremes of ugliness or beauty. Nowhere have I seen so many giants, so many perfectly-formed men and women, and at the same time so many diseased, debased, misshapen, misbegotten or crippled human beings. The girls of the middle and upper classes seemed usually very pretty, with faces fined down to an appearance of spirituality not often met with among the meat-fed robustious Londoners; and almost always with beautifully clear eyes. The shawl-wearing class, the very poor flower girls and suchlike, might have been drawn from two distinct races, their types were so distinct and opposed. Some were more distinguished in appearance than their social superiors, others again were almost incredibly debased-looking. Yet all of them had at least the attractiveness of the absolutely wild animal. I fell an easy prey to the flower girls in my first days in Dublin, allowing myself shamelessly to be blackmailed through my superstitions. The bunch of violets or sprig of white heather offered " for luck " (with the strong implication that a refusal to purchase would bring down on my head unparalleled misfortunes) were generally more than I could resist. " God bless you, sir, and keep you. I'll pray for you, sir! " was murmured as one groped in one's pocket for coins. It is a novel experience for an Englishman to be prayed for promiscuously; though possibly no one is more in need of prayers than he. When, after a time, I felt I had been prayed for sufficiently, and managed by a great effort to resist the flower girls, I used to be pursued by them with the most extraordinary flood of obscenities—obscenities used with complete disregard for their meaning, as one might misuse the *argot* of a foreign language.

FIRST IMPRESSIONS

In the mean streets of Dublin (alas, how large a proportion of the city must come under this head!) the poor people seemed always to have a frenzied look about them, even when they were sober. It was quite different from the stolid, stupid aspect of so many of the English poor. They seemed at once nobler and more degraded than their neighbours across the channel. In many ways (it is to A. E. that I owe this simile) Dublin reminds one of a drunken genius who lives in dirt and lets his children die of hunger, but is capable nevertheless of flashes of brilliance and nobility. And often, in the squalid streets, I noticed a wonderful purity in the people's eyes, a spiritual purity which perhaps accounts for their fire, their passion and their swift perceptions.

If anyone wishes to test the passion and fire of the Dublin poor he has only to stroll down some of the small streets on either side of the Nelson Pillar on a Saturday night. The scenes remind one of Hogarth's picture of Gin Alley; the quarrelling, shouting, fighting are simply indescribable. Again and again I have heard women howling and roaring at one another. I have seen them leap up into the air and actually dance with fury. One night I saw a woman who had just bought a leg of mutton for her family, rush out of the butcher's shop with the joint in her hand in pursuit of the enemy. Waving the mutton in the air like a battle-axe, she finally brought it down with a thud on the other lady's face, and the blood from the mutton mingled nastily with the claret from the victim's nose. Dozens of little barefoot boys and girls, relatives of the belligerents no doubt, watched the scene with serene faces and occasional giggles. When they are not fighting (usually at a later stage in the evening, after the pubs have closed), one can hear them weeping and wailing with a kind of Hebrew ecstacy of lamentation. All the sorrows, the agonies of the world seem to be concentrated in their anguished, distraught voices. I have often lain awake at night in my room in one of the northern squares, and heard this terrible howling. First a distant door is slammed, then there is a thud as the woman—ejected by her husband—tumbles prostrate into the street, and after that the lamentations start.

Unfortunately, the habit of getting drunk is not confined by the Dublin poor to any particular hour or day of the week, but seems to depend entirely on the state of their finances. One soon gets accustomed to meeting drunks of both sexes at all hours of the day. It is not an uncommon sight to come across a woman at mid-day lying absolutely inert in the middle of the road or pathway, or clutching at an iron railing, motionless as a statue, unable to stir. At a safe distance a little fringe of ragged children stand and gape. (Usually the children's feet are bare, no matter if the ground is frozen. As likely as not it is the proceeds from pawning their boots and outer garments which has made the celebration possible!) At last the mother or daughter of the sufferer arrives from the neighbouring slum and expostulates with the recumbent form. Nobody shows the least surprise.

The children of these very poor people reproduce the same extremes of difference as their elders. Brats of the most clodlike appearance, deformed and mis-shapen, suggesting some debased and horrible process of generation, are mixed up, sometimes in the same family, with children who might be the love-children of heroes they are so beautiful. The straight nose with fine nostrils, the short upper lip, the eyes full of fire and raillery of the latter type suggests, as far as features go, all that we understand by aristocracy. It may be that the Irish gentry of two centuries back were indiscriminately affectionate, or that the Irish race has a natural nobility which has persisted through the centuries in spite of all contamination from outside. But it is for the learned to propound theories, not for me.

The life of the Dublin streets must, I think, seem very odd and foreign and attractive to any Englishman. Sometimes on Sunday mornings one meets a crocodile of priestlings moving across a quiet square, all of them wearing scarlet-lined cassocks, with top hats on their heads, and surplices over their arms. The full-fledged priests of different ages and sizes, who are to be met all day and every day stalking up and down the central streets, giving scarcely perceptible acknowledgements to the hat-raising of the poor men, help also to lend the city its foreign air. The gigantic, dangerous-looking policemen, who stand in twos at every corner and outside every public building, are much more in evidence than the police of English towns, though I never heard a Dubliner say a bad word of them, and their civility is proverbial. The beggars, flower girls, and paper boys; the outside cars (surely the cheapest and most convenient form of "hackney carriage" anywhere to be found), all combine, with the policemen, to give Dublin its special character. I do not think I have ever seen a "D. M. P." less than 6 foot 2 in height: they strike the stranger as being, in size at any rate, a race of supermen, and their stately tread reverberates down silent streets. I have only twice encountered them in action. The first occasion was before the restrictions of martial law, requiring one to be indoors by midnight, were relaxed. I was running home a little after twelve from a friend's house near Stephen's Green, when, half-way up Harcourt Street, I was told sharply to "halt." The command was reinforced by the glint of a revolver which the peeler waved in front of him in the gaslight, pointing it at my feet. I halted duly, was told to advance slowly, and then interrogated. Apparently it was the fact that I was running which had aroused the D.M.P.'s suspicions. These, luckily, were allayed when my innocent features had been examined and I had mentioned my name, address and occupation. The peeler and I then chummed up, and we walked together for some distance, discussing the Rebellion and the behaviour of the military, for whose conduct and sagacity it appeared he had a low opinion. " They were untrained, inexperienced men," was his comment, " and some of them blagyards as well. They didn't know how or when to use their arms. . . ." We parted amid a pretty display of mutual compliments. The next occasion when I saw the D.M.P.'s at work was on " Irish Flag Day," a Sunday towards the end of June, when collections were being made for the dependants of the rebels and the deportees. Quite fifty per cent. of the people one met in the streets on this day were wearing the Republican colours, and the sums collected in the little cardboard boxes must have been considerable. I never saw anyone refuse to give. In the evening, as I was walking down Westmoreland Street at about nine o'clock, I heard a noise of singing and shouting, and, looking round, saw a procession of ragged children marching towards the O'Connell Bridge. The leader was a slip of a girl of about seventeen years old, carrying a large Republican flag attached apparently to a broomstick. Behind her came a few hundred barefooted enchantments, little girls and boys most of whom looked not more than eight years old. They were all singing " Who Fears to Speak of Easter Week " at the tops of their voices, and the effect of it (to my sentimental English mind) was moving almost to tears. The procession did not get as far as the bridge. Two peelers emerged suddenly from a side street, nipped across the road with considerable agility and began struggling with the girl with the broomstick. The sight of the Irish flag falling downwards into the dust and of a girl being roughly handled, was too much for some youths who were watching the proceedings. They rushed to the rescue, the trams came to a dead stop, there was a great deal of scampering to and fro and a few minutes of swirling confusion. However, in a surprisingly short space of time the D.M.P.'s " had the situation in hand," and the youths and the flag bearer were marched off to the police station by Trinity College. The mixture of pluck and skill shown by the police was admirable. I do not believe London policemen could have affected arrests in the face of a hostile crowd so neatly or with so little unnecessary violence.

At that time in Dublin no one could be in the city for twenty-four hours without discovering what was the general feeling of the mass of the population about the Sinn Feiners. Picture postcards of the executed rebels were displayed in almost every shop window, and their faces were gazed upon with silent veneration by the passers-by. A large photogravure of P. H. Pearse, produced by some enterprising firm, attracted crowds wherever it was displayed. Up and down Sackville Street urchins ran selling broad sheets purporting to contain "The last and inspiring speech of Thomas MacDonagh." Quaintly enough when the sale of this document had practically ceased (half the inhabitants of Dublin having bought one or more copies) its publication was prohibited and the printer summoned. So far as one could tell, except among the shopkeepers who had not received compensation for their losses and among the upper classes, all resentment against the Sinn Feiners had died away. I remember once when I was standing outside a shop in which photographs of all the Sinn

Fein leaders were on view, a very old man came and stood beside me and looked at the faces of the dead, with tears streaming down his cheeks. Suddenly he turned to me and caught my arm. "And they were all Sodality boys. . . . " he said, in a voice broken with emotion, "all Sodality boys! All near to the Sacred Heart of Jesus!"

One of the first facts which a Londoner grasps when he comes to Dublin is the fact that, for good or ill, Ireland is not in the present war. The feeling of relief experienced by the war-weary at this discovery is indescribable, and people newly-returned even from America have told me that they have had the same sensation. One such described Ireland to me as being "probably the most neutral country in the world at the present time," and I have every reason to believe him. This does not of course alter the fact that a large number of Irishmen—a far larger number than official figures will admit—are fighting. But they are fighting for the King of England, fighting in the "English army." I had an amusing illustration of this point of view in a barber's shop one day. "Well, I see we are doing rather well now in France," said the barber, with a laugh, to the man whom he was shaving.

"*We!*" spluttered the customer.

I do not think that anyone in Dublin pre-

FIRST IMPRESSIONS 35

tends that the heart of Ireland is in the war; nor (to be frank) is it possible to discover any reason why it should be. Still harder is it to discover any reason why my countrymen should expect it to be; nor why they should become so angry when they are brought in contact with evidences of Irish neutrality. The only explanation of our annoyance is to be found in the complete ignorance of the Irish point of view and of the elementary faces of Irish history which prevails on the other side of the Channel. This ignorance is nowhere shown more clearly than in the recruiting posters with which Dublin is plastered. They are veritable gems of imbecility for which it would be difficult to find a parallel. Irish farmers are asked by the " calmest confiscators" in Irish history if they can afford to have their lands " calmly confiscated " by the Germans. Other posters display an irritating facetiousness ("Join the Army, you will like it, your pals will like it, the Kaiser will *hate* it") or quotations, of doubtful wisdom, from the speeches of " patriotic" bishops; while among the pictorial masterpieces are a picture of the most dishonest type of recruiting sergeant beckoning with one finger, and a startling cartoon showing a cockney shop-assistant being given a " thick-ear " by his white-haired mother for not joining up. It is really hardly to be wondered at that these posters are used in Dublin as a vehicle for popular wit. There is scarcely one of them in all the city which has not some acid comment scrawled all over it. Dublin is a great place for political comments. On hoardings and in public places which in London are generally disfigured by stupid obscenities, one often sees long and, to the stranger, rather baffling, historico-political disquisitions. But the Dubliners seem rarely to waste their lead pencils on the merely filthy. They have too much passion, too much fire for such muddy-mindedness. I would not venture to suggest that they are more moral than their neighbours (for I am told by one of them, who ought to know, that this is not the case), but at least, so far as " the writing on the wall " can indicate it, they are less ignoble.

I do not know what view the authorities may take of such indications of popular feeling as are conveyed by processions of school children, or cheeky scrawls on recruiting posters. To the unbiassed onlooker, however, much of this appears to be sheer fun and high spirits, or as we should say " larks." Walking once up Gardiner Street I heard what sounded like the strains of " Rule Britannia," mingling with the more familiar " Tennessee." Rather surprised at this I stopped

FIRST IMPRESSIONS

for a moment and listened, and this is what the little divils were singing :—

Rule the Kayser, the Kayser rules the wurrld,
Never, never, never, never shall the Irish flag be furrled!

Yet the mind which could deduce from such an impish piece of cheek that the Irish people are " pro-Germans," or any nonsense of the sort, must surely be about as thick as the average policeman's boot. The simple fact appears to be that in Dublin the decent Irish of all classes are pro-Ireland.

The favourite game among the ragged children in the tenement districts is called, as far as I have been able to discover, " The Rebels' Camp." You see the words " Rebels' Camp " scrawled up on walls and doorways with usually a seething mass of urchins struggling in the foreground. How exactly the game is played I have never discovered; but I did not gather that it gave any special grounds for alarm to the authorities.

The locutions and pronunciations peculiar to Dublin sound very delightful to unaccustomed ears. It soon becomes evident that all Dubliners have what is known as a " civil tongue in their heads "—the famous " way wid them," no doubt. (They have other kinds of tongues, too, on occasion. In fact, there isn't much which an Irishman can't do with his tongue when he gives his mind to it.) When you go into a small shop in the evening you are greeted with the words "Good night"; and when you depart with your evening paper the proprietor observes, "Ta-ta." The minutest purchase entitles you to a remark about the weather—"It's a soft day," and so forth. The phrase "half-past eight," "half-past ten," is pleasantly shortened to "half eight," "half ten." "Ten past" any hour is always "ten-a-past." The Dublin maidservant does not ask her mistress if she shall make tea now, she says: "Will I wet the tay?" When the weather is cold or rainy she is "destroyed entirely" by the cold or rain, while to frighten or startle her is to "put the heart across her." For "jug" the prettier word "crock" is usually employed by servants, and cups and saucers are referred to collectively as "the delf." Porridge is called "stirabout," and bacon for breakfast known more precisely as "rashers." The word "rear" is always spelt in Dublin newspapers "rere." "Tuppence" and "thruppence" are pronounced more accurately in Dublin, where everyone speaks of "two-pence" and "three-pence." Empty houses are "set" instead of let. In the pronunciation of words there is a tendency to lay the stress on a different syllable from the English way—*e.g.*, concéntrate, aristocrat; and generally speaking in Irish place names the accent falls on the last syllable—*e.g.*, Dundrúm, Belfást, Armágh.

I have left it to the end of this chapter to mention what seems to me to be one of the most characteristic and noticeable features of the outward life of the Dublin streets—I mean the extraordinary number of funerals. All day, and particularly on Saturdays and Sundays, the long processions wind up Sackville Street on their way to Glasnevin. Whether it is that more people die in Dublin than in other cities, or simply that they die more expensively and with more pomp, I have no idea. But I have never before in my life been in a town where hearses and coffins and mourning coaches were so much in evidence. As the Dublin funerals have been written about by Seumas O'Sullivan, I presume they are generally recognised as a Dublin speciality. Here is Mr. O'Sullivan's poem :—

> As I go down Glasnevin way
> The funerals pass me day by day,
> Stately, sombre, stepping slow
> The white-plumed funeral horses go,
> With coaches crawling in their wake
> A long and slow black glittering snake
> (Inside of every crawling yoke
> Silent cronies sit and smoke).

Ever more as I grow thinner
Day by day without a dinner,
Every day as I go down
I meet the funerals leaving town;
Soon my procession will be on view,
A hearse, and maybe a coach or two.

CHAPTER III.

The North Side.

My first night in Ireland was spent on the north side of Dublin in a Georgian house which I have already described, and throughout my stay my allegiance to the wrong bank of the Liffey has never wavered. I was never so ill in my life as during the few weeks when I stayed in one of the low-lying streets in the direction of Rathmines. The climate of south Dublin appears to be much more relaxing and humid than the north, and is, I should imagine, much more unhealthy. The Liffey bisects Dublin almost exactly, and the two halves, not counting the suburbs, are almost exactly equal in size and in architectural interest, while the north has the advantage of being built mostly on higher ground. Gardiner Street, Sackville Street, and Capel Street rise from the river in a gentle continuous slope, so that from the top windows in Mountjoy Square, Great Denmark Street, Gardiner's Row, Rutland Square, and some of the houses in North Great George's Street, a wonderful view may be obtained of the rest of Dublin—shut in by its dark line of mountains on the one side and with the shining bay rounding off by the *presqu'île* of Howth on the other. North Dublin has alas " gone down " further even than Bloomsbury, and very few of its magnificent town houses retain more than a shadow of their past dignity except in their outward appearance. Yet Gardiner's Row, Marlborough Street, Great Denmark Street, North Great George's Street, Mountjoy Square, Gardiner Street, Upper Sackville Street, and on the other side of Rutland Square, Lower Dominick Street and Henrietta Street all contain houses of such comeliness in their proportions, of such exquisite taste in the minutæ of decoration, in moulded ceiling, chimneypiece and doorway as are rarely to be found now in London houses of the same period. I have heard it said that nowhere in Great Britain, except only by the Georgian mansions in Bath, are they excelled.

Of the public buildings on the north side, among which are the Four Courts, the Custom House, the King's Inns, and the G. P. O. (now only a shell), the most important is undoubtedly the Custom House. To my mind it is the loveliest building, architecturally, in the whole of Dublin. It was erected between the years 1781 and 1791, from the designs of James Gandon, an English architect who was brought over to Dublin by the great John

THE NORTH SIDE

Beresford, the Banker. It is perhaps to the art of Gandon more than to anything else that Dublin owes that air of metropolitan distinction which it still preserves. In spite of a number of unfortunate modern buildings, and the rather dismal and not too prosperous commercial aspect which many of its central streets and squares have acquired, Dublin is still unmistakably a capital city, and not merely a large provincial town.

The Custom House is thus described in a guide to Dublin published about twenty years after its completion:—" It is 375 feet in extent, and 209 feet in depth, having the singular advantage of four fronts, variously designed. The south, or the front opposite the river, is composed of pavilions at each end, joined to arcades, and united to the centre. The order is Doric, and is finished with an entablature, and a bold projecting cornice. The centre is enriched with a group of figures, representing Ireland and England embracing each other, and holding in their hands the emblems of peace and liberty. They are seated on a naval car, drawn by sea-horses, followed by a fleet of merchant ships from different nations. On the right of Britannia is Neptune driving away Envy and Discord. (!). On the attic storey are placed four allegorical statues, alluding to Industry, Commerce, Navigation and Riches. The pavilions are terminated with the arms of Ireland in a shield decorated with fruit and flowers, supported by the lion and unicorn, forming a group of massive ornaments. A magnificent dome, 125 feet high, rises in the centre, holding a female statue of Commerce. The statue is 16 feet high. This dome is a considerable ornament to the eastern part of the city. The keystones of the arches are decorated with colossal heads, emblematic of the principal rivers in Ireland and the counties through which they flow, well executed. . . . The interior claims equal attention to the exterior of this edifice, and must be viewed to form any suitable idea of the various apartments, &c. The great staircase, with its Ionic colonnade, is greatly and deservedly admired, uniting taste with grandeur, and possessing novelty of design. The simple arrangement of all its interior parts, with the numerous offices, is judiciously made, and well adapted to their various purposes. . . . ."

Just behind the Custom House is Beresford Place, where the Bank belonging to John Beresford was situated. John Beresford seems to have been an arch-Hun in his day, and during the rebellion of 1798 caused numbers of innocent people to be flogged and tortured. Sir Jonah Barrington records that during the outbreak " Mr. John Beresford had built a riding-house for his yeomanry troop in Marlborough Green, which has been also much used as a place for whipping *suspected* persons in, to make them *discover* what, in all probability, they *never knew*—a practice equally just and humane, and liberally resorted to (perhaps for sport) by military officers, pending that troublesome era when martial law authorised every species of cruelty.

"In Mr. Beresford's riding-house this infernal system was carried on to a greater extent than in any other place of execution then tolerated in the metropolis—to such an extent, indeed, that some Irish wags (who never fail, even upon the most melancholy occasions, to exercise their native humour) had one night the words—'Mangling done here by J. Beresford & Co.'—painted upon a sign-board, and fixed above the entrance."

The author of "Ireland before the Union" observes: "The triangle and the scourge caused the name of Beresford to be held in great detestation. He was a banker in Beresford Place; and when the insurrection burst forth, the rebels, hoping to injure him, destroyed his paper money wherever they could find it. This illogical proceeding had only the effect of enriching their foe." Beresford's Bank no longer adorns Beresford Place, of which the most noticeable feature of to-day is the battered remnant of Liberty Hall.

At the back of the Custom House, from the middle of Beresford Place, starts a broad street called Lower and Middle Gardiner Street, which terminates in Mountjoy Square. Most of the houses in this street are now let off in tenements, but many of the beautiful doorways still remain undamaged, and no doubt the interiors of some of the houses hold much that is interesting in the way of carved chimneypiece and painted ceiling if anyone were bold enough to penetrate them. Mountjoy Square itself still manages to retain a quasi-residential character, though tenements, or at least " unfurnished apartments," have gradually made their appearance along one side of it. The houses in the square, though outwardly uniform, vary considerably in their internal arrangements, some of them being much finer than others. The ceilings in No. 58 are noticeably good and are illustrated in one of the Georgian Society's volumes. Mountjoy Square is a little remote, and is one of the smallest of the Dublin squares, but it has a certain charm of its own and is so much healthier than the low-lying districts of South Dublin that it seems a pity that the tide of prosperity shows no signs of returning to it.

At the beginning of the nineteenth century this square, with the neighbouring Rutland Square, was a noted resort of the

" fashionables " (as they are called in a contemporary guide) on Sunday afternoons.

Leading from Mountjoy Square into Rutland Square is a street which, though quite short, is called at successive stages Gardiner's Place, Great Denmark Street, and Gardiner's Row. Here are a number of fine houses, including the famous Belvedere House, now a Jesuit College. Belvedere House was built about the year 1775 by George Rochfort, second Earl of Belvedere, and cost him nearly £24,000. " The ornamentation by Lord Belvedere's Venetian artists," says Mr. Cosgrave in his book on North Dublin, " was restored by the Jesuit Fathers a quarter of a century ago. The plaster reliefs on the walls and ceilings, the Bossi marble chimney-pieces, and the three rooms whose decoration was dedicated to Apollo, Venus and Diana respectively, are now in as good condition as they were a century ago, and afford the best surviving example of eighteenth century splendour in Dublin house decoration." The importation of Italian artists and decorators for work on some of the bigger Dublin houses and the prevalence all over Dublin of chimney-pieces designed by the Italian immigrant Bossi, seems to have led to a belief that all the beauties and the splendours of Georgian Dublin were due to foreign artists. But if such were the case (as Miss Sarah Purser once pointed out to me) the foreign workmen in Dublin must have numbered thousands, and of this there is no evidence. There is, on the other hand, good reason for believing that the native Dublin plasterers and designers were very highly-skilled craftsmen, though no doubt they learnt much from the Italians under whom, in certain cases, they worked. It should not be forgotten in this connection that Moira House on Usher's Island, which from contemporary accounts must have been second only to Belvedere House in its internal magnificence, was decorated throughout by an Irishman—the elder Healy.

Belvedere House looks straight down North Great George's Street, which runs steeply down from Great Denmark Street into Parnell Street. North Great George's Street, though at first glance of comparatively modest appearance, is really one of the finest streets in the whole of Dublin. Some of its empty houses, which I used to amuse myself by going over, almost took one's breath away, their beauties were so unexpected. Like most Dublin houses, they seem to have been built mainly with a view to entertaining. The ground floor and first floor consist entirely of great reception rooms, the rest of the house, the bedrooms and servants' accommodation, being to modern ideas rather inadequate and out of proportion. In some of the houses the grand staircase ends at the saloon, and the only way up to the bedrooms is by a dark stone continuation of the back stairs. These saloons, however, are so well-proportioned, so nobly adorned, that one can hardly grumble at the generous and hospitable instincts of the people for whom the architects designed them. Among the most interesting of the houses in North Great George's Street is Kenmare College (No. 35), but there are several others of almost equal beauty. As a rule the Georgian houses in Dublin (at all events in North Dublin) look their best when they are empty. Modern Dublin ideas of wallpaper, furnishing and so on often strike one as having failed to progress since 1880. At No. 20 North Great George's Street, Sir Samuel Ferguson, the poet, came to live soon after his marriage, and we are told that in this house he and his wife "practised an open, generous and delightful hospitality towards everyone in Dublin who cared for literature, music, or art."

Returning to Great Denmark Street, it is but a step to Rutland Square, which still presents a dignified appearance though much of its original character has probably been destroyed by the trams which surge along the Sackville Street side of it and by the modern Gothic church which stands at the corner of what used to be called Palace Row. It is in this Row, at the upper end of the Square, that the finest of its houses—Charlemont House—is situated. Charlemont House is a large stone-faced mansion, standing some distance back from the rest of the Row, with a graceful sweep to its front door. It is now the General Register Office for Ireland, so that the fabric, at all events, is assured of preservation. The house was designed by Sir William Chambers for James Caulfeild, first Earl of Charlemont, and was built or begun in **1773**. "The virtuous and accomplished Charlemont," as Macaulay describes him, seems to have been the leading figure in the brilliant Dublin Society of his day, and his house is said to have become " a centre, like Holland House in London, of politics, society, art and letters." His art collections, long since dispersed, were remarkable even in an age of great collections. Before his Dublin house was built he travelled on the Continent, and particularly in Italy, and he lived for some years in London, where he became the intimate of Johnson, Goldsmith, Boswell and others of their circle. The younger Grattan wrote of him as being " the most accomplished man of his day, the most polished and the most agreeable." Another contemporary, Edward Malone, observed: "Lord Charlemont is the politest man I have ever seen. In him politeness is no effort. It arises naturally and necessarily from his warm and affectionate heart." I take the following passage from one of the Georgian Society's volumes: "In the eighteenth century the figure of Charlemont stands out unique among the Irish peers as an accomplished nobleman who, by his cultured tastes, his patronage of art and letters, his keeping in constant touch with the ablest men of his day, greatly elevated and inspired the tone of society in the Irish capital. He was not a great man, but with a moderate understanding, patriotic views, a mind improved by education and enlarged by travel, he was so alive to his responsibilities as a great Irish landowner that he became prominent in political movements. He lived in an age when great social position carried much political weight." Lecky says of him that "He had personal qualities of a kind which often go further in politics than great brilliancy of intellect; and he was one of the very few Irish politicians who had never stooped to any corrupt traffic with the Government." Most of his art treasures were housed in his villa on Dublin Bay—Marino, at Clontarf—where he caused the lovely Casino to be erected in the grounds. This property was sold by the family in 1880 to the Christian Brothers, and the pictures were then dispersed.

Charlemont seems to have had many engaging personal idiosyncracies. He detested new clothes, especially new hats which his family had to use various stratagems to induce him to wear. He was so hospitable that no one knew who would dine at his house, " for he asked whom he would on the instant." But of all his peculiarities, surely the one which endears him most was his taste for breakfasting alone. Even after his marriage, we are told, he continued his practice of having breakfast by himself, with a tame mouse as his sole companion!

Running parallel with the west side of Rutland Square is Lower Dominick Street, which contains many beautiful houses. This street is older than either Rutland Square or Mountjoy Square, and one of its best houses is No. 20, which belonged at one time to the Hon. John Claudius Beresford, famous for his torturing proclivities, and subsequently to Lord Ffrench. It is now used as a school, but its exceptionally fine hall and staircase are still in a good state of preservation. At No. 45 Sheridan Lefanu was born, and Anthony Rowan Hamilton lived for a time at No. 5. Dominick Street is now a dismal thoroughfare, which it is to be feared does little credit to the Corporation of Dublin. The poorest of the Dublin population—and are there any poor in the British Empire as desolate as the Dublin poor?—pack themselves as closely as human sardines into many of its crumbling mansions. One of these tenements I was solemnly assured (though I am unable to credit it) housed no less than one hundred and seventy-three persons! When it is realised that the rather meagre sanitary arrangements which were deemed sufficient for a nobleman's household at the end of the eighteenth century are all that now exist, some conception may be formed of the revolting condition of these human rabbit-warrens. I was pointed out the " shoots," on each floor, through which the inhabitants of the house were accustomed to empty their slops and garbage down into an alley.

Even sadder in some ways than the decay of Dominick Street is that of Henrietta Street, a short street of once palatial dwellings which begins with a piece of waste land covered with tins and old boots and terminates in the King's Inns, one of the handsomest of Dublin's public buildings. The houses in this little street (which is about as long as Great Stanhope Street, Mayfair, and from the architectural point of view even finer) are for the most part tenements with broken windows and swarming doorsteps. Yet it was in one of these houses—at No. 16— just a century ago, that the fair and frail Lady Blessington was presented to her husband's guests. When the Lord Mountjoy of those days first became a widower in 1814 the funeral of his wife was conducted with unexampled magnificence and cost a fabulous sum. Two years later he became Earl of Blessington, and soon afterwards brought his second wife to his Dublin house. She was the widow of a certain Captain Farmer who had been killed in a drunken brawl in the Fleet prison. When the couple went to live in London, Lady Blessington's house became the centre of artistic and literary society, until her unbounded extravagance necessitated her flight to Paris, whither she went in the company of Count D'Orsay. We have Mirabeau's assurance for the fact that this lady would draw wit out of a fool, and though no one nowadays reads her books, the charm of her dazzling personality still lingers and is fragrant. No. 11, another fine house, has associations with Henry Boyle, Earl of Shannon, who died there in 1764.

The appearance which these two streets must have presented in the latter half of the eighteenth century, during the time of Dublin's greatest prosperity, when every family of gentle folk had carriages and horses in their stables, and when money was spent in the town with reckless prodigality, is not difficult to imagine. If one dips into any history of Ireland one generally gets the impression that throughout the ages the country has always been miserably indigent.

But the streets of Dublin to-day proclaim in themselves that the impression is false, if one takes the trouble to examine them. During almost the whole of the eighteenth century, and particularly at the end of it, in the lifetime of Grattan's Parliament, Irish money was being spent in Ireland, and the general state of prosperity, at all events in Dublin, must have been fairly high. Absolutely indigent farmers cannot pay rents, as was discovered in the nineteenth century, and unless their property had been capable of yielding them a considerable income Irish landowners could never have built themselves town houses like private palaces, and costing in some cases as much as £80,000. But Dublin is a city whose most noticeable feature is the magnificance of its domestic architecture. The life lived in these great houses must have been expensive, and the amount of money in circulation in Dublin must at one time have been very large. At the same period also (and before England ruined them) Irish industries must have boomed. Ruined mills and factories are now a picturesque but saddening feature of the valleys near Dublin; and the old "Linen Hall" is another indication of bygone commercial activity—relic of an industry once flourishing and a source of wealth, which was strangled by maladministration.

One of the most revealing things about

Dublin (in regard to its past splendours) is the elaborate nature of the stabling, outbuildings, servants' cottages, and so on, which are to be found at the backs of almost all the houses. A house without a stable and coach-house at the back of it is a rarity in Dublin. Nowadays the majority of these stables are in ruins, but some of them have been made rainproof and converted into cottages, and are let off in tenements like the houses to which they belong. Some again, in an intermediate stage of decay, form a refuge for unfortunate squatters. Once, when I was being shown over an empty house in Dominick Street by an elderly manservant, I remember looking out of one of the top windows across the curious expanse of outbuildings, coach-houses and so on which lies between Dominick Street and the backs of the houses on the western side of Rutland Square. A lane bisects this desolate tract littered with ruinous masonry, and in the middle of it I noticed a curious building of grey stone, tall and bare, and containing a number of narrow windows. "Ah, they were great times when these were all gentlemen's houses," said my guide. "The stables and cottages you see down there were filled with horses and grooms and coachmen in those days, and there used to be pretty green shrubs standing on each side of the stable gates. My father has often told me how the servants from these houses used to sit and drink porter and play cards in that little lane down there. That big stone building you are looking at," he went on, pointing to the place which had already puzzled me. "used to be a swell publichouse a hundred years ago, where all the upper servants about here used to go at night. Quite a famous place it was at one time. Now any rooms in it which are habitable are let off in tenements, like these." The Leinster family have a town house in Dominick Street, which was occasionally used as a residence by members of the family until recent years; and I believe there is at least one other family in the street which still clings to its old home.

The principal place of amusement in North Dublin towards the end of the eighteenth century was the "Rotunda," in Rutland Square. This handsome, circular concerthall, built in 1755 from the designs of Richard Johnson, is still in use, though the Cinematograph has taken the place of the fashionable balls and routs formerly held there. The decorations both inside and out are very handsome. The frieze of draped ox-skulls which adorns the exterior was designed by Flaxman. The hall is not without its historic associations, for it was one of the meeting places of the Irish Volunteers of 1782, of whom the Earl of Charlemont (whose house at the top of the Square overlooks it) was General in Command. The Rotunda adjoins the Rotunda Hospital, which is said to be the oldest maternity hospital in the Three Kingdoms. The main block of the hospital buildings is by Cassels, and the beautiful little chapel has been attributed to Gandon. A hideous new wing in red brick with yellow stone facings is on a par with other eyesores of modern construction which are unfortunately to be found in Dublin.

Among the other public buildings on the north side are the Four Courts, a noble edifice built of melancholy grey stone, with a beautifully-shaped dome rising from the midst of it. It stands forlornly on the Quays between the Grattan and the Church Street bridges, surrounded by squalor and decay. Dublin public buildings appear to have been plumped down anywhere, wherever there happened to be a plot of ground to build them on, and none of them seems to have been able to do anything to " raise the tone " of the neighbourhood in which it found itself. The Four Courts was erected during the Irish Independency. Cooley was the first architect, but Gandon took charge of the building in the middle and superintended its completion. The big granite G.P.O. in Sackville Street is now little more than four bare walls with empty windows in them, but the Ionic portico with its six fluted columns supporting the pediment, remains more or less intact, and shows that the building must have been handsome enough. It dates from 1818—a little later than the clumsy Nelson Pillar (imitation of the one in Trafalgar Square) which stands opposite it.

The Pro-Cathedral in Marlborough Street —a street running parallel with Sackville Street on the eastern side of the Nelson Pillar—probably dates from about the same period as the General Post Office. It is a massive, undistinguished granite building, like a kind of bastard Greek temple. In a country like Ireland, where everything is on short commons except Horse-Racing and the Catholic Church, it seems rather odd that the Pro-Cathedral should present such a poverty-stricken appearance. But its interior decorations are very meagre and tawdry, and lack entirely the sumptuousness which characterises most modern Catholic cathedrals on the Continent. Its chief glory is its famous choir, which Mr. Edward Martyn founded and endowed some years ago, and of which Mr. Vincent O'Brien is the Choir Master. In Marlborough Street, almost opposite the Pro-Cathedral, stands Tyrone House, a fine stone mansion built in 1740 for the first Earl of Tyrone, and now used as Government Offices. In Mary Street, a busy shopping centre on the west side of the Pillar stands Langford House, one of the oldest of the great Dublin houses. It was built between the years 1697 and 1712 by Paul Barry, Keeper of the Pipe or Great Roll of the Exchequer. Henry Ingoldsby, of Cartown, Co. Kildare, who became Earl of Langford, bought the house from Barry, and it remained in his family until, in 1809, it was sold to the Corporation for the offices of the Paving Board. During the occupation of the Paving Board the exterior of the house was deprived of much of its interest by being refaced with brick. It now forms the premises of Messrs. Bewley & Draper. Close to Langford House is St. Mary's Church, which faces Stafford Street, where (at No. 44) Wolfe Tone lived for some time with his parents. St. Mary's has interesting connections with Swift, Sheridan, and other great names. Sheridan was born at 12 Dorset Street, not far off, and was baptised in this church.

One of the most magnificent as well as the most forlorn of the great houses of Dublin is Aldborough House, which rears its noble façade from amidst a wilderness of little streets near the Amiens Street Railway station. It is said that there were never any entertainments in this mansion which the first Earl of Aldborough nearly ruined himself to erect. It was sold to the Government within a few years of its completion; and is now used by the Post Office authorities. This enduring monument of human vanity never had any history, and even at the time when it was built, its situation can scarcely have been agreeable, though no doubt the view of Dublin Bay obtainable from its upper windows must be very fine on a clear day.

What exactly were the causes which led to the decay of North Dublin (and indeed, in a less degree of South Dublin too) is a matter for more learned persons than myself to discuss. Perhaps the Rebellion of 1798 was the first blow, and there seems little doubt that the Act of Union inflicted irreparable injury on the prosperity of the whole city. The writer of a Guide to Dublin, published as early as 1811, refers to the matter thus:—" On the 1st January, 1801, the Union Act became an operative law, Ireland being united to England. The Imperial united Standard was on this occasion first displayed upon Bedford-Tower, Dublin Castle. The removal of the Parliament from the metropolis has proved very injurious to the trade of the city . . . ." That " injury " of some kind was done to the prosperity of Dublin, beginning at the time of the Act of Union, is obvious to any visitor who spends a week in the city and keeps his eyes open. If English government in Ireland is to be judged by its effect on Dublin (a point which I do not affirm, because I do not know enough about it), then that government must assuredly be condemned by all Irishmen and all Englishmen too, as an unqualified failure. How different from Dublin is the aspect of a city like Trieste, for example, and other cities on the Dalmatian coast which are supposed to be groaning under the tyranny of Austria. The Austrian Government may be very tyrannical —of that I have no knowledge either way— but at least it is plain to the traveller that commercial prosperity goes hand-in-hand with it. The races subject to Austria may be down-trodden, but wherever the K. K. Government has left its mark we find progress, trade, good order, good roads, and good education. And much may be forgiven a tyranny which is efficient.

CHAPTER IV.

South Dublin.

Such signs of comfort and prosperity as are to be noted to-day in Dublin (and alas, they do not amount to very much) are almost all to be found on the south side of the Liffey. I fancy the more elegant Dubliners rarely cross the O'Connell Bridge unless they are on their way to a race meeting in the Phœnix Park or being carried, toes turned up, upon their final journey to Glasnevin. On the south side are to be found Dublin's two most famous squares, Merrion Square and Stephen's Green; the Castle, that mournful pile of offices; the two Protestant Cathedrals, St. Patrick's and Christchurch; almost all the theatres, the picture galleries, the National Library, the University, the Bank of Ireland (housed in what were formerly the Irish Houses of Parliament), and most of the principal shops.

Westmoreland Street, which runs from the O'Connell Bridge to College Green, terminates with the irregular classic pile of the Parliament buildings on the one side and Trinity College on the other. The long façade of Trinity facing College Green, with the Provost's house standing detached at the far end of it, is handsome and unpretentious and well in keeping with the purpose for which it was designed. Perhaps if one could only get a good view of it (and the same applies to the Houses of Parliament opposite, and, indeed, to very many of the principal buildings in Dublin) one would discover still greater architectural beauties. Unfortunately the tramcars and all the undistinguished movement of the streets at this point conspire in some way to diminish the effect which the buildings ought to make. If only the Houses of Parliament stood absolutely detached from other buildings; if only College Green were twice as broad, the difference would be amazing. One thinks of many quite small towns in France and of the way space has been made use of in them to lend the architecture an air. Nevertheless, "bang on the street" as it is, the group of buildings now used by the Bank of Ireland has a most original and charming appearance, particularly under a clear sky. The Westmoreland Street front with its columns in the Corinthian order (the rest of the building being in the Ionic) shows Gandon at his best; but the earlier south front, with its handsome colonnades, which was designed by another architect, is equally original and happy. In the middle of College Green, facing Trinity, is an excellent statue of Grattan by Foley, who is also responsible for the attractive statues of Burke and Goldsmith, which stand one on each side of the entrance to the University. The buildings of Trinity, the Chapel, Dining Hall, Library, and so on, are nearly all of granite, and on the whole strike one as being more dignified than elegant. The modern Engineering School, however, combines both these qualities. The dining hall is bare and a trifle sombre after some of the college dining halls of English Universities; and the appearance of the great library seems in some ways to belie its date (1732), though this may perhaps be due to the recent raising of the roof and building in of the colonnades. One of the chief treasures in the library is the famous " Book of Kells," an illuminated copy of the Four Gospels dating from the seventh century. Unlike some other antiques which one has examined with an earnest but unvailing desire to achieve intelligent interest, this survival of ancient art is a thing of extraordinary beauty which no one should visit Dublin without seeing. But the library itself, in spite of all its interesting " exhibits "—or perhaps because of them— strikes one as being a mere mausoleum of books in which no one would care to read who could possibly go elsewhere. Very different in this respect is the National Library, which forms part of a group of buildings lying between Merrion Square and Kildare Street, comprising the National Galleries, Leinster House (now the home of " The Royal Dublin Society "), and the Museum. The Library and the Museum are usually entered from the Kildare Street side (though there is a small gateway into Leinster Lawn), and group themselves one at each end of the grey granite mass of Leinster House. Their architecture is ornate but scarcely inspired, and in the gardens which separate them, with her back to Leinster House, stands perhaps the very worst statue of Queen Victoria which is to be found in the British Isles. The guide-book says it has been nicknamed " Ireland's Revenge."

The atmosphere of the National Library, though naturally less cosmopolitan, is almost as delightful as that of the British Museum reading-room. Whenever I have been there to read, which is very often, it has always been crowded. The staff are efficient and helpful, and the whole place has about it that air of vitality which comes from constant use. Mr. Magee, the Sub-Librarian, who is also a distinguished man of letters, is always ready to put his wide scholarship at the disposal of those who need his help, and there can be few people in Dublin connected with writing who have not at one time or another gratefully availed themselves of it. Of all the Dublin institutions which I have explored the National Library seems to me the one most admirably managed and most clearly of " national importance."

Leaving the library and going through the little side door into Leinster Lawn, one finds oneself in a moment in Merrion Square. My eye for acres is untrustworthy, but I fancy this oblong must be larger than any of the famous London squares, though it is not so large as Stephen's Green. Its central gardens, however, unlike Stephen's Green, are unfortunately not open to the public. The houses which compose its three sides (the fourth is almost entirely taken up by Leinster Lawn and the National Gallery) are good examples of late eighteenth century architecture, and appear to be occupied exclusively by physicians, nearly all of them complete with knighthood. Whether the knighthoods are achieved first and are followed by migration to Merrion Square, or whether they are wafted from the Castle immediately on the signing of the lease, is a point about which one perhaps ought not to speculate. The fact remains, nevertheless, that a brass plate unadorned by the imposing prefix looks quite distinguished by its rarity.

At No. 1, formerly the home of Sir William Wilde, the youthful Oscar graced his parents' parties in the eighteen-seventies; Daniel O'Connell, the Liberator, once resided at No. 58, and Sheridan Lefanu, that curious literary figure, lived at No. 70. The finest of the Merrion Square houses is said to be Antrim House (now Nos. 33 and 34), which was completed early in 1778 from the designs of George Ensor, and soon became famous for the brilliance of the entertainments held there. Nowadays Merrion Square has little interest of this kind, and the long lines of brass plates remind us too painfully (no libel is intended) that the worms await us all. To-day the most important of its houses is undoubtedly the Plunkett House, No. 84, which was bought some years ago by subscription and presented to Sir Horace Plunkett as a centre for the various organisations to which he has devoted his life. To visit the Plunkett House is quite a spiritual adventure. Once inside the doorway the visitor's senses are charmed by a subtle aroma of poetry and produce. Intellectuals of all ages and sizes—but each enthusiastic face fired by a cheery idealism—flit up and down its broad staircase: and high at the top of the house sits Mr. George Russell busy editing *The Irish Homestead.* "Co-operation," word more blessed than Mesopotamia to Mrs. Malaprop; co-operation, that spiritual antiseptic which, like some patent tooth-paste, kills the germs of political futility and decay in less than thirty seconds, impregnates the air in the Plunkett House with its life-giving ozone. I must confess I do not know anything about co-operation (except perhaps that the eggs it sells are sometimes no better than they should be), but its spell is so potent that I am already a postulant co-operator, waiting impatiently to take the final vows!

Upper Merrion Street, which leads up from Merrion Square into Ely Place, is now chiefly devoted to Government offices and to hospitals. It contains some fine houses, of which the largest is Mornington House (No. 24), where the Duke of Wellington was born: it is now the home of the Land Commission. Going on into Ely Place (that pleasant *cul-de-sac* in which for ten years Mr. George Moore lurked behind his green front door, an earnest seeker after the *frisson* of conversion) and turning to the right down Hume Street, we find ourselves in Stephen's Green, the centre of modern Dublin. The gardens of this vast square have been turned, through the generosity of a wealthy Irishman, into what must surely be one of the loveliest small parks in the world. In all weathers and in all seasons it has a beauty which indeed changes constantly, but never grows less. A lake, stocked with many different varieties of water-fowl, winds across it; and there is a little bridge at one end of the lake, close by a rockery and cascade, where on summer evenings the contemplative may linger. If the Green is a seductive place in July, it is no less so in December. At five o'clock say, on a winter afternoon when the light is fading, and the setting sun flushes the clouds with a misty red glow, when the shop windows begin to glitter and the bare branches of the trees are outlined in black, making a delicate tracing against the pale sky, it is like a glimpse of some subdued fairyland. I have never seen any twilight like the twilight in Ireland: it is small wonder that the mystery of it pervades so much Irish verse.

From Stephen's Green thoroughfares, some of greater some of less importance, branch out in all directions. From one end of it Grafton Street, that thronged and shop-lined promenade, winds down into College Green. There are no trams in Grafton Street, and of all the Dublin shopping centres it is the most prosperous, the most full of movement. At the same time, it must be admitted that the description "the Bond Street of Dublin" which has been applied to it, is a little misleading.

Opening off the Green on the western side are several little streets which have now gone down in the world—King Street (where the Gaiety Theatre is), York Street, Cuffe

Street. York Street has several interesting associations. That unhappy poet, James Clarence Mangan, lived here for a while; and No. 37 was at one time the home of one of those fine crusted characters of which writers of Irish memoirs describe so many examples— the Rev. Charles Robert Maturin. Maturin, like others of his countrymen, seems to have devoted so much genius to his personal idiosyncracies that he had but a mediocre residue of talent left over for his books. He was the author of a play called "Bertram" and several other plays and novels; and was also a fashionable preacher. The following account of this eccentric personage is taken from the *Dublin University Magazine* (1858):—"He was eccentric in his habits almost to insanity and compounded of opposites; an inveterate reader of novels, an elegant preacher, an incessant dancer, which propensity he carried to such an extent that he darkened his drawingroom windows and indulged during the daytime; a coxcomb in dress and manner, an extensive reader, vain of his person and reputation, well versed in Theology, and withal a warm and kindhearted man. Among his other peculiarities he was accustomed to paste a wafer on his forehead whenever he felt the *estro* of composition coming on him, as a warning to the members of his family that if they entered the study they were not to interrupt his ideas by question or conversation."

Stephen's Green itself is, naturally enough, very rich in historic associations and contains a number of exceptionally fine houses. At No. 86, a stone-fronted mansion which now forms part of the Catholic University, the famous Buck Whaley (or Whalley) once resided. "One day, for a bet, he threw himself out of his drawingroom window into a barouche, as it rattled past, and kissed its fair occupant." He was sometimes called "Jerusalem Whaley," from another bet he made to *walk* to Jerusalem within a short period, and play ball against its walls. Another Stephen's Green character was Francis Higgins, the "Sham Squire," who lived at No. 72. He was intimate with Whaley, Lord Clonmell, and John Claudius Beresford. Higgins seems to have been a parti-coloured blackguard of singular success in his day. Beginning life in a cellar in Dublin, he became first an errand boy, then a waiter in a porter house, afterwards an attorney and Justice of the Peace. One of his early exploits, from which he derived his nickname, was to pose as a man of property in order to gain the hand of a wealthy heiress, Miss Archer. This unhappy lady, who always objected to the match, died of shame soon after her husband's true character was revealed. Higgins was imprisoned for this adventure, but like the famous prisoner of Nantes, made love to his gaoler's daughter and was soon at large again. From this point his fortunes took a turn and he rose by rapid stages. He became an attorney, pimp, informer, proprietor of a gambling hell, Government toady, Justice of the Peace, amateur impressario (he had a passion for the theatre), and proprietor of a newspaper (the *Freeman's Journal*) which was the subsidised organ of Lord Buckingham and every Viceroy from the Duke of Rutland in 1784 to Lord Hardwicke in 1802. The legacy of hatred which " the Castle " has inherited, however much we may deplore it, is not after all so hard to understand. The crowning villainy of Higgins' career was the betrayal of Lord Edward Fitzgerald, for which he was paid a thousand pounds (thus getting the bulge on Judas). Although Higgins left much of his money to charity, a fact which may indicate certain qualms of conscience, he appears always to have carried off his iniquities with an air. Some personal recollections of Higgins, supplied by an aged sexton of St. Werburgh's Church, are recorded in an entertaining volume from which I take the following passage:—" The appearance of the Sham Squire was a familiar object to me in my early days. He was daily to be seen with Buck Whalley upon the Beaux

Walk, in Stephen's Green. This walk ran along the north side of the Green, between an ugly wall, five feet high, and an impregnable haha, or dyke, on the other side. The appearance of the Sham Squire constituted in itself a very remarkable object, and now, after the lapse of nearly seventy years, it is strongly impressed on my memory. He wore a three-cocked hat, fringed with swan's-down, a canary-coloured vest, with breeches to match, a bright green body-coat, with very sharp tails, spangled with highly-burnished buttons, and he was the only buck in Dublin who wore gold tassels to his Hessian boots; violet gloves concealed his chubby fingers, richly decorated with rings. He wore no neck-handkerchief, but a stiff stock, fastened by a diamond brooch, elevated still more his already pompous chin. All the canes used in those days were nearly as tall as a footman's, and reached as high as the shoulder, in order to display the richly-embossed gold head. People as they passed would nudge each other, and view him with a mingled feeling of awe and interest. Even few of those who were acquainted with the Sham Squire would venture to salute him as he daily displayed his person, dressed in the pink of fashion, along the Beaux Walk in Stephen's Green." Higgins died in 1802.

Sir Walter Scott who visited his son in Dublin in 1825 and dined with him at No. 9

Stephen's Green, a magnificent town house which in those days had sunk to being used as garrison lodgings, described the Green as " the most extensive square in Europe "—I know not with how much truth. But beauty has nothing to do with mere extent, and however the Green may compare in size with foreign rivals, I do not believe that it can be surpassed by any in attractiveness. To-day it has a suspicion of that inimitable down-at-heel air which is perhaps peculiar to Dublin. It keeps its self-respect and dignity, it has successfully avoided progress, but it has also manifestly " seen better days."

There are many fine town houses in South Dublin, most of which are now used as business premises or as Government offices. One of the most grandiose of them all is Powerscourt House in William Street. This stone mansion was built between the years 1771 and 1774 for Richard Wingfield, Viscount Powerscourt, at a prodigious cost. It had a fairly long history for an Irish nobleman's town house, remaining in the possession of the family till 1811, when the fourth Viscount Powerscourt was no doubt glad to get rid of it to the Crown for £15,000. It was first of all made the office of the Commission of the Stamp Duties in Ireland, but has long been turned to mercantile uses. As is the case with so much of the architecture of Dublin, the exterior of Powerscourt House loses greatly in effect from the fact that owing to the narrowness of William Street it is impossible to get a good view of it. Set in such cramped surroundings it looks a little clumsy and top-heavy. Standing alone in a park, however, with a setting of trees and rising ground at the back, it would probably look magnificent. It would almost seem as if the architect had designed the house without considering anything about the site it was to occupy, except only the length of frontage at his disposal.

Clonmell House in Harcourt Street, of which the Municipal Gallery now occupies the larger half, is another fine house, though its exterior is plain and built of brick like the majority of Dublin houses. Its most famous occupant was John Scott, Earl of Clonmell, from whom it takes its name. Scott was an *arriviste* barrister, famous throughout Ireland for his effrontery and coarseness, who, like the notorious Lord Norbury, bullied and "shot" his way up the ladder of legal preferment. His method of speaking was described thus by Grattan:—"He struck his breast, slapped his hat constantly, appealed to his honour, and laid his hand on his sword." We are told that he required " a couple of able-bodied lacqueys to carry him to bed every night "; and that " his size increased so much through his indulgence in drink that he broke the springs of two carriages through his excessive weight." As he drew a salary of £15,000 per annum, we may assume that Dublin " money offices " were in an even more flourishing condition before the Union than they ever became after it. This impressive personage died in 1798; and he seems from some of his charges to juries and from his private diary, some portions of which have been published, to have been neither such a fool nor such an unmitigated knave as is often assumed. There is a cunning, which occasionally rises to wisdom, in several of his aphorisms:

"*Observation of the World.*—That the sayers of good things are usually the doers of very little good. *Bon mots* and good actions do not go together.

"*Manners and Customs.*—Live constantly at home; as much as possible take your exercise at home; never be seen in the streets; and when in public always dressed in full, and pay the utmost attention to your appearance. Carry your station constantly about with you with the decency and port that belong to it. It makes the meanest character passable and dignifies the greatest. When you dine alone let it always be a fast day in eating and drinking, for it is most beastly to stuff and guzzle alone.

"*Persuasion.*—Never attempt to bully your superiors into conviction; woo them, and sometimes hurry them.

"*Knowledge of the World.*—Avoid intimacies. Never be intimate with any man or woman but for the purpose of answering your purposes upon them; and never suffer either, upon the same rank with you, to take liberties or to be intimate with you. I never suffer an injury from anybody but an intimate; and every painful moment of my life, every mischief done to me, has arisen from intimacy—treachery, envy, ingratitude, resentment, arising from intimacy. Suffer no man to come so near you that you cannot call him ' Mr.' with propriety."

Lord Clonmell considered bishops to be generally humbugs and hypocrites, believed musicians to be usually fools in mind and conduct and thought Oliver Cromwell the character best worth imitation. His Diary, cynical as it is and full of rather pompous good resolutions about drinking water with his meals, reveals a man who, if indecently material and unscrupulous in many respects, was nevertheless a man of rare sagacity. The last part of the Diary deals with events immediately before the Rebellion. The author of "Ireland before the Union" remarks: "To Lord Clonmell had been early divulged the dark designs of the Government to foster the Rebellion, in order, when the country was prostrate and exhausted from loss of blood, to carry the Union. . . ." The following entry, dated 1796, shows that the accomplishment of legislative union was, thus early, part of the Ministerial scheme:—

"Saturday, 23rd April, 1796, St. George's Day.—Lord Camden, with a vast concourse of people, nobility, gentry, and rabble, attended at Ringsend, with music and cannon; and a public breakfast given by the Governors of the Grand Canal at the opening of the new docks, and sailing into them a vast number of ships and small boats. The Judges and Bar left the Courts to attend so new and splendid a sight. But what will become of all this expected commerce in Dublin if a Union is to take place? . . ."

As introductory to the next entry in the Diary, it should be observed that Lord Moira had, on November 22nd, 1797, delivered a memorable protest in the British House of Lords against the system of maddening torture which was goading the country into rebellion. "Thirty houses were often burnt down in one night; men were made to stand barefooted on a pointed stake; they were half hanged, and often threatened with a repetition of the cruelty; every man was at the mercy of a soldier's caprice."

"Feb. 13, 1798.—The arrival of Lord

Moira in this country to throw it into confusion, as apprehended, by encouraging the malcontent Papists and Presbyterians. N.B.—I think my best game is to play the invalid, and be silent; the Government hate me, and are driving things to extremities; the country is disaffected and savage; the Parliament corrupt and despised. Be discreet and silent."

"Probably it helps to cover a multitude of Lord Clonmell's sins," says the author of "Ireland before the Union," "to record that he was no co-operator in the policy of the bad statesmen who, in the Irish reign of terror, daily goaded the people to madness. Some passages in Grattan's life throw light on remarks in Lord Clonmell's private diary. His nephew, Dean Scott, told Mr. Grattan, ' that Lord Clonmell had gone to the Lord Lieutenant and told him, that as they knew of the proceedings of the disaffected, it was wrong to permit them to go on—that the Govenment, having it in their power, should crush them at once and prevent the insurrecrection. He was coldly received, and found that his advice was not relished.'"

Lord Clonmell's house in Harcourt Street was furnished with great luxuriousness; every room is said to have been hung with Gobelins tapestry, and his library contained over 6,000 volumes.

Perhaps what was formerly the most

famous of all the great Dublin houses is now the one which of them all presents the most lamentable appearance of decay and desolation. This is Moira House in Usher's Island, on the southern bank of the Liffey, near Kingsbridge station. To-day, the long, low, dismal-looking building shows not a trace of its original splendour; indeed anything more forlorn and dejected than its present aspect it would be hard to imagine. Since 1826 the house has been used as an "Institution for the Suppression of Mendicity," and nowadays the most pathetic of human waifs and outcasts creep to it for their doles. The old man who showed me round, pointing to a bust of the Duke of Northumberland which stood in the hall, remarked with deep feeling: "He was a great man, sir, he was. He was the very *founder* of mendicity!" For some reason which I have been able to discover—perhaps it was in a kind of puritanical frenzy—before the house was turned to its present uses, not only was the upper storey removed, but all the superb interior decorations were destroyed, and its gardens abolished to make way for offices and out-houses.

No great house in Dublin seems to have played a more brilliant part in the social life of the city than Moira House. It was originally the seat of the Rawdon family,

Earls of Moira, and until the death of the first Earl in 1793, it was the scene of constant and magnificent entertainments. Among the artists employed to beautify the interior was the elder Healy, father of that Robert Healy whose self-portrait in crayons is one of the most delightful things in the National Portrait Gallery. John Wesley visited Lady Moira at Moira House in 1775, and " was surprised to observe though not a more grand, yet a far more elegant room than any he had seen in England." The room he referred to was an octagon room with a window the sides of which were inlaid with mother-of-pearl. In 1777 Charles James Fox was introduced here for the first time to Henry Grattan: and it was at Moira House more than twenty years later that the unfortunate Pamela first heard the news of the arrest of her husband, Lord Edward Fitzgerald.

Other fine houses in South Dublin are Northland House in Dawson Street; Mespil House in Mespil Road, famous for its plastered ceilings; and Molyneux House in Peter Street. This house, which dates from 1711, was leased by Philip Astley " the equestrian " after the Molyneux family had migrated to Merrion Square, had an interesting theatrical history under various managements and finally, after a number of vicissitudes, sank to its present humble condition, that of a common lodging house.

There are many more houses of architectural or historic interest in Dublin than those I have named, and indeed to explore them all would necessitate a visit to the city not of months but of years. Small as it actually is in extent, the streets of Dublin seem interminable to the explorer. The streets immediately adjoining the Castle, including Werburgh Street, with the curious St. Werburgh's Church; the two great Cathedrals of Christchurch and St. Patrick; the "Liberties"; the Coombe and Weavers' Square, once the headquarters of the weaving industry introduced by the Huguenot refugees—chapters or indeed whole volumes might be written with any or all of these for a subject. As I sit in my window and write these lines looking down over Dublin and across to the hills beyond, I can recall no other city which I have ever seen which conceals so much romance and beauty beneath an outer surface so forbidding.

CHAPTER V.

Hills and the Sea.

If we had to pick and choose among the natural beauties of the world as we know it, I suppose most of us would name hills and the sea as being the loveliest examples of God's handiwork. A city built like Dublin at the inmost end of a deep bay and shut in on one side by a line of the most alluring hills to which men's eyes were ever lifted, would seem therefore singularly blessed in regard to its situation. It is small wonder that Dubliners love their bay, and can scarcely speak of their mountains without emotion. Even the poorest slum child in summer can walk out to Irishtown or Clontarf, or along the South Wall, and paddle to its heart's content; while for a few pence the whole sweep of Dublin Bay, a stretch of something like twenty miles, is within everybody's reach. Opinions are sharply divided as to which arm of the bay is the more attractive, the one which terminates in Howth which stretches out like some couchant tiger carved in rock, or the other side which ends in Dalkey with its island "kingdom," and includes Kingstown, Blackrock and Merrion. The Kingstown side, if the visit is to be prolonged for more than a day, has the advantage of being close under the hills. Gaunt Three-Rock rises up at the back of you with its attendant peaks and within twenty or a dozen miles of the coast is to be found some of the wildest scenery which exists anywhere in the British Isles. Except, perhaps, in the Department of Ardèche in the Cevennes, I do not think I have ever seen a more desolate stretch of country than these deserted uplands. The whole district lying roughly between Blessington and Bray is practically uninhabited, and it was in this deserted mountain wilderness that the Rebels of 1798 took refuge.

The hills round Dublin are not high, Three Rock Mountain, one of the chief of them, being no more than 1,585 feet. But further south, some of the peaks in Wicklow reach a greater altitude. Mullaghcleevaun is 2,783 feet, while the mountain mass of Lugnaquillia, still further to the south, rises to 3,039 feet at its highest point.

The hill which is most accessible to Dubliners is Mount Pelier which is little more than an hour's easy walking from the Rathfarnham tram. On your way there you pass the burnt-out shell of a little place called Mount Venus, which will be very familiar by name to all Mr. George Moore's readers.

Nothing now remains of the house except bare walls, and most of its demesne has been ploughed up and sown by the neighbouring farmer, to whom no doubt the place belongs. But the view from the rough stone steps of the house is surely superb. I do not believe that any villa overlooking the Bay of Naples could have a more enchanting prospect. I have spent many a blazing afternoon lying in the long grass by the front door of this pathetic ruin, or sitting on the rough-hewn steps, unable to leave the place. No sunlight, however serene, frightens away the ghosts who haunt Mount Venus. I do not think they are malevolent ghosts, simply they cannot bring themselves to go away. They cling to their grove of black ilex trees, bent by the wind, and look down, as the traveller does, over the bay's wide expanse and across the hazy sea. No views in or near Dublin, however clear the air may be, are ever very brilliant. There is no brilliance in the Dublin sky, even in midsummer. Even when there are no clouds and no mists, everything is softened. That dark green landscape cut into little squares which is the " plain of the birds," never loses its subdued tones, and Dublin itself is never a city of shining roofs and towers. A blue-grey veil seems to hang over it perpetually; it is a grey town. As for the sea, it is a pale green, or a pale blue flecked with white, a northern sea, untamed, mysterious, knowing nothing of the deep ultramarine of the Mediterranean. Only the green of the hillsides is vivid in the Dublin landscape; and the only point which really catches the light and reflects it is the Hill of Howth. Howth will lie basking in the sun like a great cat when all the rest of the bay shudders in gloom. I have often been rain-bound in the hills and looked across at Howth to see it shining and at peace.

In a field close to Mount Venus there is a giant cromlech, which is an excitement to antiquarians; but I must confess I never went to look at it, the long grass was too comfortable. The steep, grassy knoll of Mount Pelier rises at the back of Mount Venus, and is but a few minutes climb from the battered gates of its demesne. This hill, from which another unrivalled view may be obtained of Dublin Bay, is surmounted by a little ruinous stone house with walls of tremendous thickness, which is generally known as the " Hell Fire Club." In the exposure of its position and in its unutterable bleakness (particularly in winter, or on a stormy day) it reminds one for all the world of a miniature Wuthering Heights. The building is said to be the remaining portion of a hunting lodge built about the year 1725 by William Connolly, M.P., Speaker of the Irish House of Commons, and it is said that the members of this notorious

Hell Fire Club used occasionally to meet in it. The club is supposed to have been established in Dublin about 1735, by Richard Parsons, first Earl of Rosse and the painter, James Worsdale, who was Deputy Master of the Revels. The Dublin headquarters of the Club was at the Eagle Tavern, Cork Hill, and its proceedings are supposed to have been livened by every sort of blasphemous naughtiness and debauchery. A picture of several of its members, painted by Worsdale, hangs in the National Portrait Gallery, and (except as an indifferent painting) need not shock anyone. The debauchees represented are Henry Barry, fourth Lord Santry, Colonel Clements, Colonel Ponsonby, Colonel St. George, and Mr. Simon Luttrell, of Luttrellstown, afterwards the first Earl of Carhampton.

On the way back to Rathfarnham from Mount Pelier on either side of the road are clear rock-strewn streams flowing down through green valleys, their course here and there interrupted by ruined mills now overgrown with ivy and looking as venerable as ancient abbeys. Yet scarcely more than a century ago the wheels were turning, and the mills were giving employment to workpeople whose descendants are now very probably in America. At one of these ruined mills, close to Mount Venus, which I once stopped to explore, a labourer informed me that the paper for the Irish bank notes used to be made. But the industry was killed by excessive taxation. The duties became so high that at last " they used to have to steal the paper through the fields " in order to avoid them! In this neighbourhood there are no less than five ruined paper mills within an area of one square mile.

There are a number of pleasant little towns and villages lying just outside Dublin, on the plain which intervenes between the mountains and the bay—Dundrum, Stillorgan, Churchtown, Carrickmines and Leopardstown (famous for its race meetings) being among them. Near Churchtown is the famous Cuala Press, under the management of the Misses Yeats, from which a number of beautifully-printed books have been issued, to be snapped up promptly by collectors. The Irish would seem to possess a certain natural delicacy of touch in everything which is done with the hands which makes them peculiarly successful in the decorative and applied arts. In the eighteenth century, as I mentioned in an earlier chapter, many of the elaborate plaster ceilings, chimney-pieces and such like, which form the glories of Dublin house decoration, must have been the work of Irish artist-craftsmen. To-day the tradition is continued in the work turned out by the Cuala industries (including the Cuala Press), the Dun Emer industries, the various schools of Irish lace-making, and also by the guild of stained glass window makers of which Miss Sarah Purser is the founder and Honorary Secretary. The " Book of Kells " is the supreme example of what an Irish decorative artist has produced, but the tradition has lingered on since the far-off days of the seventh century and not the least important part of the work done in different ways by Miss Purser, the Misses Yeats and others, would seem to be the discovery and encouragement of some of that native talent which would otherwise be lying fallow.

The various little seaside towns between Dublin and Dalkey which are linked up by the tram-line, as well as by the railway, have all a distinctive charm and character of their own. The suburb of Sandymount which seems to be a little out of the main stream has a contemplative " residential " air. Further round the bay is Blackrock, where the best sea-bathing is to be had in summer; and further still is Kingstown which flaunts an unnatural prosperity that one instinctively resents. This is due in part no doubt to the mail service between Kingstown and Holyhead which lends the town an appearance of bustle and efficiency; but in the summer months it goes in as vigorously for " attractions "—Bands, concerts and such-like—as any English watering place. Many Dublin people come out to Kingstown for July and August. Indeed the Dublin habit of spending a summer holiday in some outlying suburb which can be reached in a few minutes by a local train—Kingstown, Dalkey, Killiney, Howth or Malahide, or wherever it may be—seems rather quaint to English ideas. To a Londoner it is rather like going to Kew or Richmond for an August holiday. On the other hand the bay of Dublin is so lovely that there is little point in paying expensive railway fares simply in order to escape from it. Bray, which some guide book or other describes as " the Brighton of Ireland," and which is about twelve miles out of Dublin, is one of the most detestable, lugubrious spots I have ever been in. Kingstown is infinitely preferable to it, and so also is Killiney. Killiney, which is separated from Kingstown by the wooded hill of Dalkey and its projecting cape, is one of the most favoured of all the seaside " resorts " near Dublin. There is something almost Italian about its tranquil bay, the dark trees on the hill slopes below Dalkey on the left-hand side and the little island kingdom of Dalkey with its ruined chapel lying out in the dreaming sea, just beyond the point. Whenever I have been to Killiney there has been a curious softness in the air. The place is very sheltered, and roses linger in Killiney gardens far on into November. It is small wonder that so many opulent Dublin families have built their villas there.

Of the inland beauty spots resorted to by Dublin holiday makers, Lucan and Leixlip, some miles up the valley of the Liffey are perhaps the most attractive. Lucan is reached by an electric tram from the park gates. The tram passes through the pretty village of Chapelizod with its evocative name (Chapelle Isolde). This village has, I believe, the distinction of being Lord Northcliffe's birthplace. The tram to Lucan proceeds with great circumspection, and the journey—through a rather dull countryside—takes about an an hour. Lucan is a pretty town on the Liffey, well girt with trees and centring round a church whose spire looks as though it might have been erected purely with a view to the " composition " of the picture. The place, to my eyes at all events, had little to differentiate it from any large English village, and no doubt it is unusually prosperous and a trifle sleek for Ireland. There is a big hotel and sulphur spa just outside it, where visitors may drink the waters (playing golf, of course, in their spare moments). By diving down into a tunnel within the hotel grounds one emerges inside the Vesey demesne, on the banks of the Liffey. The walk through the park to the far lovelier village of Leixlip takes about twenty minutes. The reaches of the Liffey below the famous Salmon Leap are as trim and well-behaved as the Upper Cherwell at Oxford; but at Leixlip the river becomes wilder. Than Leixlip I never remember to have seen a lovelier village. A tributary stream runs into the Liffey here; and Leixlip Castle stands on a wooded knoll above the meeting of the waters, a meeting surveyed more closely by an old stone gazebo built at the water's edge at the termination of a long riverside walk. If I was trespassing I must beg the owner of the castle to forgive me, but to walk up the stream to the waterfall I chose the castle side of the river and found a gravel path overhung by trees leading along by the river's brink, with decayed iron seats set here and there along the route, showing that the path had once been more carefully kept. At the waterfall the Liffey boils over from a considerable height in a brown cascade (the colour of pale porter) amid scenes of great beauty marred only by a large modern building, a mill or power station, which stands at the top. The path continues beyond the waterfall, through pleasant woodland scenery, till it reaches what is said to be the oldest bridge in Ireland. Not far from here is the great house of Castletown with its 365 windows, the seat of the Connolly family; and also the village of Celbridge, familiar to readers of memoirs and to lovers of Swift. His Vanessa

(Esther Vanhomrigh) lived at Celbridge Abbey and conducted her highly intellectual *amitié amoureuse* with the Dean on a seat under the rocks by the Liffey's edge. Leixlip, though popular enough in summer, is comparatively off the main track for Dubliners, constituting more of an " expedition " than a visit to one or other extremity of the bay, to Dalkey or to Howth.

I was for long unable to make up my mind as to which of these last two spots I preferred, but after six or seven months I think that I love Howth the better. It is much wilder and less genteel in appearance than Dalkey; less prosperous and populated, and the Hill of Howth is incomparably beautiful. The tramway to Howth passes through the suburbs of Clontarf (famous in Irish history for the battle fought there between Brian Boru and the Danes) and Dollymount. Clontarf is where Charlemont's country house, Marino, stands, with its before-mentioned Doric Casino, Chambers' masterpiece, hidden among the trees. Dollymount, the terminus of some of the trams, is a place much frequented in summer by the working-class population of North Dublin who take their children to paddle there in the trickle of water which at low tide separates the North Bull sand bank from the mainland.

It would take many days to explore the

whole of Howth; the Baily Lighthouse which stands on a grass-covered rock, sticking out into the sea at the south-eastern end of the promontory; the great rocky hill of Shiel Martin which overlooks it; the demesne of Howth Castle and the down-at-heel little town which sits gaping at its vast but half-deserted harbour. I have often been to Howth, but I fear incurable laziness has always prevented me from carrying out my good intentions in the matter of climbing and exploring. But, indeed, every part of the Howth excursion, from Clontarf onwards, is delightful. As the tramcar follows the bend of the bay the view across to Kingstown with the grey Dublin mountains frowning behind it in a long dark line is curiously exciting. Twilight seems to linger among them. The twilight which all the Dublin poets write about, there it is. Glints of sunshine occasionally illuminate the rich greens of their lower slopes. In the middle distance, as one looks back, one sees Dublin lying at the end of the bay— a grey, misty expanse, broken here and there by towers, domes and chimneys, and the trellis work of the masts and spars of the sailing-vessels in its docks. As the tram, after crossing the narrow neck of land which separates Howth Hill from the mainland, runs into the town, one gets a view of the sea and coast on the further side of it, towards

Malahide and Portmarnock, with Ireland's Eye in the foreground and the larger Lambay looming mysteriously in the distance out of the tranquil sea. Howth has a harbour much too big for it. Its great stone quays were built at the beginning of the nineteenth century for the mail service, but the harbour was so badly engineered that it soon proved useless for the purpose for which it was intended, and about a million pounds of public money was accordingly wasted. A corner of the big harbour is now used by a fleet of fishing smacks, and it is a pretty sight to watch these leaving their moorings one after the other, making for the sea under the steam of their curious little engines, and then setting sail in a half-moon formation towards the north-eastern fisheries. I don't think I have ever seen so many sea-gulls as there are at Howth, though these birds frequent the whole of Dublin bay (and even Dublin itself) in extraordinary numbers. At Howth they literally cover the harbour and hover in a dense cloud over the big fish troughs on the sea wall, where the women and girls stand in their tall boots and sou'westers sorting the catch. I have spent many an afternoon watching them. Sometimes one of the girls would throw out a herring for fun, and long before it fell into the water it would be swooped upon, caught, snatched from beak to beak and scrimmaged for like the ball in a Rugby football match. The great sleek gulls look curiously sinister as they hover over the fish tubs with their long, well-fed white bodies, outstretched evil beaks and feet extended and close together, like a boy in the act of making a " flat " dive. They are much handsomer birds when they stand up in a long row on some pointed roof or sea wall, motionless as china images; or when they walk along one after another, in solemn procession. There is something wild and insatiable, like the sea itself, in their greedy screaming when they fight over the food that is thrown them; or when, unappeased, they fly even over the roofs of Dublin, going sometimes as far inland as Mountjoy Square or Stephen's Green. There are always a number of gulls in Stephen's Green, and always one of them poised, motionless, on the helmit of King George II., making that kingly effigy seem more ridiculous than ever. At Howth the screaming of the gulls is so continuous that it contrives to give the whole town an atmosphere of eerie harshness and dissatisfaction.

The demesne of Howth Castle to which the public are admitted on at least one day a week, is quite unlike any other private park that I have ever seen. The higher part of it, near the steep cliff which is covered with rhododendrons, is a kind of ordered wilderness of winding paths, climbing and twisting up the sides of the hill, and so thickly overgrown with trees that it is easy to lose one's way among them. In June the rhododendrons are an unforgettable sight, an intoxicating riot of colour which the tropics could scarcely surpass. It was on a blazing summer afternoon, I remember that I first explored these enchanting walks in the company of a friend who had volunteered to pilot me. After considerable exertion we followed up one of the paths to the top—it was like a long green tunnel—until we emerged into the open on the hillside and sat down to rest in a clump of cool bracken. Before us lay the whole stretch of Dublin Bay, with Dublin a grey blur in the distance.

"Tell me, what do you think will be the future of Dublin?" I asked eagerly. "Do you think the whole place will revive again, after the re-opening of the Irish Parliament?" (I had only been in Ireland a few weeks, it must be remembered, and had not yet been cured of asking questions of this kind.) "Dublin will never 'revive,'" said my companion, in a voice of sepulchral gloom. "Living in Dublin is like living in the years immediately before the end of the world: you wonder if it will just last your time. The real life of Dublin is extinct, so it can have no future. Cork will have a future, perhaps; Belfast will certainly have a great future;

Dublin will grow more and more decrepit. There is a blight over it; its air is poisoned; the real Dublin people have a worm gnawing their vitals which makes them incapable of ever doing anything. All the people who make a name in Dublin are northerners, or men from the South and West. In politics few of the men who really matter in Ireland are Dubliners, and it is the same in literature and in everything else. Dublin absorbs people and then rots them gradually through contact with its own ineradicable rottenness. The best of the Sinn Feiners, even, were not really Dublin men. Dublin is a diseased place: it's a pity a great deal more of it wasn't blown to bits in Easter week!"

I protested vigorously. Granting, under pressure, the rottenness and decay, I could see in imagination travellers from all the world coming to stay in gigantic palace hotels as yet unbuilt. Long before Dublin sank to its lowest ebb it would be "discovered." Ritz-Carltons would rise among its ruins, prosperity would return even as it has returned to Italy. "You English are all the same. Shaw was perfectly right. Your Broadbents exploit everywhere and everything!"

"Not at all," I rejoined hotly. "I am merely arguing from the situation of Dublin, of which nothing can ever deprive it. Dublin will be saved by its mountains and its bay;

and also by its past. It will be saved, in spite of itself, by the pressure of the world's interest and admiration. . . ."

"Exploited by foreigners, you mean!" Perhaps it was what I did mean. In any case we left it at that.

CHAPTER VI.

The Municipal Gallery of Modern Art.

The Municipal Gallery of Modern Art, at present temporarily housed at No. 17 Harcourt Street, owes its existence to the enthusiasm and energy of the late Sir Hugh Lane. The long and complicated story of Lane's difficulties in getting the Dublin Corporation to allow Dublin to reap the benefit of his generosity, and of his subsequent more violent grievances against the London National Gallery, have been told too often to need recapitulation here. At the moment when I write this the whole matter is once again being thrashed out in the newspapers, in connection with the unwitnessed codicil by which Lane sought to give effect to his dearest wishes for the enrichment of Dublin. As the Municipal Gallery stands at present, it is shorn of the most interesting and important of the pictures which originally hung there. Before these lines are in print I greatly hope a decision in regard to these treasures will have been arrived at; and that their ultimate return to Dublin will have been secured. But even without the Manets, the

Renoir, the Daumier and the other masterpieces which rightly belong to it, the collection in Harcourt Street is well worth visiting. The little gallery has an extraordinarily pleasant atmosphere about it; it is cosy and welcoming; it is like the house of a friend. And, unlike its more august companion in Leinster Lawn, it seems really popular with the Dublin public. People " drop in " casually; servant girls on their evenings out spend an hour there between 8 and 9 in preference to the more exciting " pictures " of the cinematograph; it does not depend for its appreciators on the floating population of visitors and tourists. It has been said over and over again that Dublin is apathetic about its Municipal Gallery, that no one in Dublin cares a rap about the pictures, that the institution is regarded as a kind of White Elephant, an unwelcome and useless gift. So far as I can tell, after visits extending over six or seven months, this is untrue, and particularly so as regards the Irish art student whom the gallery is primarily intended to benefit. There is, however, it must be admitted, a certain section of the educated, the professional and the middle classes in Dublin, who regard all the arts as a waste of money and actively resent them in consequence. (All the " provinces " throughout the world contain people who think like this: it is, in its

THE MUNICIPAL GALLERY 103

very essence, the "provincial point of view.") But I doubt very much whether it really predominates in Dublin, as some distressed Dubliners allege. In any case, I am convinced that the Municipal Gallery is much appreciated by working-class people, and if the National Gallery should ever become democratic and popular one feels that it will be largely due to the existence of the gallery in Harcourt Street. The two galleries are interdependent, and from the educational point of view there can be no doubt about the importance of the Municipal Gallery.

To me there has always seemed something curiously seductive about the Gallery in Harcourt Street. A kind of fragrance clings to it; it is still haunted by the ghost of its founder —an "enthusiastic" ghost if one can apply such an adjective, in this connection—and the touch of the vanished hand is apparent everywhere. I think the personality of few men recently dead remains more beautifully enshrined in the memory of his friends than does that of Sir Hugh Lane. I can think of hardly anyone whom I regret more keenly not to have seen and spoken to. His portrait in Orpen's "Hommage à Manet" which I first saw I think at the New English Art Club, always fascinated me curiously; and the same fascination is exercised in Sargent's portrait, a photograph of which I have looked at constantly in a friend's house. The chief quality in the face seems to be an extraordinary "fineness," a fineness which shows in every feature, in the ivory skin, the dark eyes, the fine, almost silken hair. And the expression which Sargent has caught and rendered is full of that intense, rapturous interest in life and appreciation of beauty which so often compensates those whose fate it is to die young. "Lane's permanent memorial," wrote Mr. Thomas Bodkin soon after the "Lusitania" disaster, "is to be found in the collections he got together, the galleries he supervised and in the magnificent gifts he so constantly made to an unappreciative public. Camille Mauclair, the French poet and art critic, described his power of forming and arranging representative and scholarly collections of pictures as an art in itself—*l'art de donner un musée*. . . . His project for the establishment of a Municipal Gallery was his dearest ambition. He made many sacrifices to attain it, and the failure of his schemes proved cruelly disappointing. His appointment to the Directorship of the National Gallery last year (1914) gave his generosity a new outlet. The city was already, before his appointment, deeply indebted to him for many wonderful gifts to both the Gallery in Harcourt Street and the one in Leinster Lawn. After his appointment his desire to benefit became unbridled. Last year alone he gave us pictures of immense value and significance by amongst others, Beerstratin, Desportes, Espinosa, Piazzetta, Bassano, Romney and Nanine Vallain. He was never adequately thanked. His motives were constantly maligned by men who did not imagine that generosity and patriotism could be so independent of profit."

The circumstances surrounding the birth of the Harcourt Street Gallery were described as follows in *The Athenæum*, by Mrs. Duncan, the present Curator, who was one of Sir Hugh's most active supporters in all his projects for the benefit of Dublin: "Shortly afterwards (1904) the magnificent collection of the late J. Staats-Forbes came into the market, and Sir Hugh conceived the ambitious project of founding a Gallery of Modern Art in Dublin, with the best of these pictures as a nucleus. With his usual eagerness he at once arranged with Mr. Staats-Forbes' executors that the pictures he selected should be exhibited in Dublin, and offered to the Irish public at a specially favourable price. At the same time he persuaded a number of distinguished painters and sculptors to present examples of their work to the proposed gallery and himself promised to give to it his own private collection of modern pictures. This he did, and the

Municipal Gallery of Modern Art which was opened in an old Georgian house in Dublin in 1907 contains a hundred pictures, statues and drawings presented by him, or about a third of the entire collection. In addition he lent to this gallery a number of important examples of the work of Manet, Renoir, Monet and other painters which he had purchased at the Staats-Forbes sale, and promised them as a gift if steps were taken to provide a permanent building to house the collection. . . . . For six years no steps were taken in Dublin, and finally Sir Hugh himself came forward and, with the aid of a number of friends, offered a building free of cost to the city, provided a site were found for the gallery." Mrs. Duncan continues:—" Of the miserable controversy that ensued and that resulted in the removal of the promised pictures, I do not now wish to speak. But those of us who knew his generous spirit knew that in a very few years all bitterness would have been forgotten, that Dublin would have had its Gallery, and that its chief ornament would have been the 'Lane Conditional gift.'"

These words were fully borne out by the codicil to Sir Hugh Lane's will, in which his wishes are precisely expressed: he wanted Dublin to have the pictures after all. He had always set his heart on giving them to Dublin,

THE MUNICIPAL GALLERY 107

and any bitterness which may still have remained in his mind about the rejection of the Bridge site was completely swamped by the much greater bitterness he felt against the London National Gallery for not hanging the French pictures which he had lent them for exhibition. It is interesting to read the comments of two distingished Frenchmen on the pictures which—if they were not at first properly appreciated by the Dublin Corporation—were treated still more shabbily by the experts in Trafalgar Square, who have now so tardily begun to appreciate them. This is what M. Salomon Reinach, the head of the St. Germain Museum in Paris, wrote to the late Mr. George Coffey :—

" Dear Sir—Many thanks for that most interesting illustrated catalogue. I am quite surprised to find that so many of our good modern pictures have found their way to Dublin, including that admirable woman of Corot, the two Puvis, and the Manets. I must say that one feels a little ashamed not to have secured the Eva Gonzales portrait for our own French collection. However, it is pleasing to think that those works of French genius have been brought to a country where France is generally appreciated, and which seems, even in pre-historic times, to have entertained close intercourse with Gaul. Dublin and Berlin are now the two only towns

—beside French-speaking towns like Brussels—to possess a good collection of French nineteenth century art. It is true that the nineteenth century was the great epoch of French art; people are only just beginning to realise that, and it is a good fortune for Dublin that a clever amateur understood that before many others, who pay mad prices for second-rate Italians of the quattrocento, because it is the fashion. Monet's 'Waterloo Bridge' and Manet's 'Concert' will outlive many so-called Botticelli's.—Yours very sincerely,
"Salomon Reinach."

The other letter is from M. François Monod, one of the keepers of the Luxembourg Gallery, to Miss Sarah Purser:

"Dear Miss Purser—I was very glad to hear lately from my friend, Sir Hugh Lane, that public-spirited people are making in Dublin a move to get a gallery specially built for the municipal collection of modern pictures. The collection is very well known now in Europe and America as a wonderful one. The choice set of Corots, the delightful series of smaller pieces by Constable, the priceless 'Twilight in the Forest,' by Courbet (Courbet's best wooded landscape, in my opinion), Rousseau's pathetic and unforgettable 'Moonlight,' Troyon's 'Cutting Brushwood' (an exceptionally fine instance of Troyon's landscape), 'Winter at Vetheuil,' which is unquestionably one of Monet's masterpieces; Manet's portrait of Eva Gonzales and 'Concert aux Tuileries,' which the Luxembourg and the French public shall ever regret not to possess—not to mention so many other excellent works—were selected with exquisite taste and rare luck. I do always remember how deeply I was impressed two years ago when visiting Dublin's Municipal Museum for the first time. To be sure there is no such gallery of contemporary art—I mean a modern public collection entirely built up pursuant to the same principles as a gallery of ancient art—that is to say, without regard but to the artistic value and intrinsic quality of the pictures. There is none like the Dublin one either on the Continent, or in Great Britain, or in the United States.

The more does one regret that such treasures should be unsuitably housed—despite of a careful and skilful hanging—poorly exhibited on the whole, on account of insufficient light, fine and charming though the old Dublin mansion may be. Then I must acknowledge I could not but remember with fear the risks of fire to which the collection is permanently exposed; one does feel very uncomfortably anxious about such conditions. We are eagerly looking forward to the quick and successful completion of a plan in which not only Dublin and the Irish nation, but French art is concerned.

"With kindest regards, believe me, dear Miss Purser, yours very sincerely,
"Francois Monod."

Before leaving the subject of Sir Hugh Lane I must quote from an appreciation of him published by one of his English friends, Mr. Lewis C. Hind, which appeared in the *Daily Chronicle*:—"Single-minded in his love and pursuit of art, a gatherer-in at Lindsey House in Cheyne Walk, of rare and beautiful things, patron and encourager of young artists of talent, he also showed himself to be a great organiser, with wonderful powers of persuasion, the aim always being the founding of galleries and the acquisition of pictures for them. It would need a book to relate all this great Irishman did for art in Ireland. The collection of pictures he lent, gave, and cajoled painters to give, to form the Dublin Municipal Gallery, made it, the Luxembourg excepted, the finest collection of modern pictures in the world. His unerring taste chose the best examples, and it was the grief of his life that his offer of the collection to Dublin, provided a proper gallery was built, was not accepted. It is a

THE MUNICIPAL GALLERY 111

long, sad, complicated story. Let us hope that Dublin's memorial to her illustrious son will be the building of this gallery on which he had set his heart." This is how Mr. Hind sums up the character of his friend. "Very simple in his manner of living, keen as a boy about any little adventure or excursion, shy, yet bold, pliable, yet of iron will, quiet yet wild for excitement, and as pale and calm, though inwardly in a ferment, over a shilling game of cards as when he was bringing off a colossal coup. Enormous sums and great masterpieces passed through his hands, but he never hoarded money; yet he practised absurd little economies. Money, in little sums, was something to be careful about, in huge sums it was simply the wherewithal to acquire more pictures, or *objets d'art*, or jewellery. He was the supreme connoisseur. Where did his knowledge come from?—not from study, not from books—he rarely read them. It was an instinct with him—genius. As Chopin took to music, he took to pictures from childhood; he handled them, loved them, cleaned and restored them, adored them, and when he died there passed away not only a vital and lovable man, half Don Quixote, half a shrewd business brain, but the greatest art connoisseur in the land or in the world."

Shorn of its chief treasures, the Harcourt Street Gallery, delightful as it is, does not constitute an adequate monument to the memory of the man thus described, nor one by which he would have cared to be judged. One can well believe that there were questions of personal feeling involved, besides his great love for Ireland (and bound up with it) which induced him, in drawing up the codicil to his will, to try to make arrangements for the Harcourt Street collection to be reconstituted in the way which he had originally planned. Handsome as the house in Harcourt Street undoubtedly is as an example of Georgian domestic architecture, it is to be hoped that the removal of the pictures to a new gallery worthy to hold them will not be long delayed. About a quarter of the canvasses are permanently invisible, and to see many of the others it is necessary to dodge into a corner to avoid the glare on the glass. But no skill on earth can turn a dwelling-house, however magnificent, into a picture gallery, and considering the difficulties involved in an attempt to do so, it is remarkable how much has been accomplished.

The first room one enters, on the ground floor, is principally filled with works by Irish painters, of which the most important are the five pictures by Nathaniel Hone. Except by hearsay I was entirely unfamiliar with Mr. Hone's painting until I came to Dublin. It is very broad, impressive, almost rugged.

There is something primeval about his morose landscapes and coast scenes. In such a picture as "The Donegal Coast" (to my mind the loveliest of the five), he looks directly at the face of Nature as if unconscious or oblivious of human life, and the scene is rendered with a massive simplicity and grandeur. This seascape has also a kind of sternness which would seem to be one of the painter's most essential and intimate qualities. He is at his best in painting his native country, and his picture of Venice, a subject for which his natural austerity is unsuited, does not seem to express the artist's personality, and gives therefore an impression of comparative failure. Orpen's lovely still-life "China and Japan: Reflections" is among the other memorable things in this room. Lavery's hard "Portrait of an Austrian Lady" will not please this painter's many admirers who have seen more happily-inspired examples of his work, though it necessarily attracts attention. Miss S. C. Harrison's portrait of herself with her mouth open has a curious, naïve charm which is difficult to analyse. Of Mr. George Russell's three pictures, the one I liked best was "On the Roof Top: Moonlight," though its appeal seems purely literary.

It is in the back room on the ground floor that the chief treasures of the whole collection

—as it exists to-day—are to be found. I refer to the seven little Constables which hang on a screen at the end of the room by the window. Of the seven I think the one I prefer is the " Weymouth Bay." It is impossible to look at it without a feeling of exhilaration. The day is cold, and bright—the month is April—and there is a hard, gay wind from the land which is flecking the sea with foam and driving the little sailing vessels out across the bay. (I remember just such a day as this in Brittany, at St. Nazaire—the same brisk wind, the same bracing bleakness and bright unwarming sun.) The picture is extraordinarily evocative, it gives one a kind of nostalgia for things and places which perhaps in this life one never knew. One gropes in one's mind for memories which constantly elude: now one has it, now it is gone. There are days when I love the " Elder Tree " or the " Cloud Study " which hangs next to it the best, but usually it is the " Weymouth Bay " which I most enviously covet. In his large pictures, such as the " Hay-wain " and others in the London National Gallery, Constable has never appealed to me very much, certainly never as much as the elder Crome. But I can scarcely think of any pictures in the world which I would sooner possess and spend my life with, than the three I have mentioned out of the examples of his art which hang in this Gallery.

THE MUNICIPAL GALLERY

There are a number of French pictures in this room, of the Barbizon school. There is a Harpignies, hard, simple, unpretentious yet achieving all that it attempted, so that one could never grow tired of it—perfection even in a small thing can never tire; a curiously tender landscape by Daubigny; a number of small Corots; Troyon's "Cutting Brushwood;" a Degas (rather uninteresting) and two characteristic pictures by Monticelli. There are also several Mancinis here and in the passage outside, for which I must confess an imperfect appreciation. Power seemed to me their outstanding quality, and power, however displayed, arrests attention. But something more than mere power is required for the production of great art, and it is just this "something more" which Mancini seems to lack. He is as brilliant as you please; so is Cinquevalli when he stands on one toe and balances six billiard balls at the end of his cue. The small picture by Mauve called "The Shower," a group of peasants plodding along a country road and holding up forlorn umbrellas, is one of the pleasantest things in the room. I was disappointed in Claude Monet's famous "Waterloo Bridge," but I must confess that I have always admired this painter with difficulty, even at Rouen where his work may be seen at its best. In the "Waterloo Bridge".

he seemed to me to be repeating himself in the stalest and dreariest of cliché phrases. It is almost as if he had a formula for "impressions," using the same formula for London that he used for Rouen, so that in his London paintings you do not get London seen through the artist's eyes, but merely a repetition of his formula. The Le Sidaner, to my mind, suffers from being "saturated with wistfulness"—if I may borrow a graphic phrase. It is twilight in the little country town, the yellow lights from the big house shine out through the gloaming—a pretty picture enough, but it scarcely gives one a thrill down the spine. Fantin-Latour's "Blush Roses," with that stolid heavy beauty of their's which seems to match so well with a mahogany dinner-table or the poetry of Matthew Arnold, would be preferable to live with. Other pictures in this room which I remember are a pleasant little garden scene by Roelofs called "Noorden," Wageman's "Sur la Plage," an attractive exhibition picture of a kind which had a great vogue on the Continent ten or fifteen years ago; an invisible portrait by Blanche; an equally invisible coast-scene by Charles Cottet and a still-life by Mlle. Karpeles.

On the staircase which leads to the landing which serves as a Sculpture Gallery, and thence to the first-floor rooms, there hangs an

THE MUNICIPAL GALLERY 117

interesting and representative series of portraits of leading Irish men and Irish women. I have noticed that these portraits attract much attention from visitors to the gallery, who gather round them in groups and excitedly discuss the originals. A portrait of Lady Gregory by Mancini hangs facing the staircase, and on the left-hand side on the way up, there are portraits of Dr. Douglas Hyde, Standish O'Grady, Jane Barlow, Mr. George Coffey and others. On the second half of the staircase hang pictures of Katharine Tynan, Captain Shaw-Taylor, in pink; Mr. Birrell, Sir Horace Plunkett, W. E. Fay and J. M. Synge. These portraits are by various hands, and include a whole series by Mr. William Orpen. Others are by Mr. John B. Yeats, Count Markievicz, Mr. Dermod O'Brien and Miss Purser. Count Markievicz' portrait of Mr. George Russell does not seem a particularly successful effort; but it is unfortunate perhaps that it should hang next to Orpen's portrait of himself.

The Sculpture Gallery is small but contains several Rodins, including a copy of the Age d'Airain and a portrait bust of great interest of George Bernard Shaw. Rodin has seen Shaw as only a few of his contemporaries have seen him. Beneath the familiar mask of buffoonery he has detected wisdom, sincerity and a great kindliness and pity. It is

Shaw the prophet and philosopher whom Rodin has portrayed; perhaps this is the way in which future generations will see him too.

The front room on the first floor, the great saloon of Lord Clonmell's house, is an exceptionally fine room with an elaborate gilded ceiling; it is a room which seems to keep the pictures in their place. Millais' "Lilacs," a picture of a horrid little girl who holds out her apron in which some cut blossoms have been heaped, looks obviously ill at ease at having been brought down from the nursery. I think it is the worst Millais of his "bad" period which I have ever seen. There are three pictures by Watts, two portraits not among his best, and one of his allegorical pictures, "Faith, Hope and Charity," which in spite of the changes of fashion still compels a certain reluctant admiration. On the same wall there is a large Albert Moore, called "Azaleas." An appreciation of the art of this painter is perhaps an acquired taste: I must admit that I have not yet acquired it, though I can perceive the beauty of the drawing of "Azaleas."

The most important picture in this room is Whistler's lovely "The Artist's Studio." There is also a small portrait of Walter Sickert by Whistler hanging on the same screen, together with a beautiful, unobtrusive

THE MUNICIPAL GALLERY 119

wintry landscape by the late H. G. Moon, and rather an uninspired " October Morning " by Stott of Oldham. Facing Watts' big portrait of Mrs. Louis Huth is a tall, empty portrait of " The Artist's Wife " by Lavery. She is seen painting at an easel with a big palette in her hand. A large white umbrella shelters her from the sunlight which fills the picture. Other things I noticed in this room were two landscapes, one by Wilson Steer, the other by Professor Brown; Spencer-Stanhope's curious Pre-Raphaelite Venus (a plaintive-looking girl with her head on one side, presumably bewailing the fact that the painter has allowed her only one breast); and a fine " Venetian Scene " by James Holland, whose dates are given as 1800-1870, and whose art was unfamiliar to me.

In the large room at the back which opens out of the saloon, almost the first picture which meets one's eye is Mr. Augustus John's masterly " Portrait Study." It is not on the same level as the " Smiling Woman," nor, to my mind, as interesting as the earlier " decorative groups " in which the influence of Puvis is still discernible, but it is eminently characteristic of the painter, and portrays one of his favourite types. On another wall the usual pretty and rather fatuous Tuke reminds us gratefully of the fact that this collection is singularly free from works of the kind with which the majority of small public collections both in England and in France are apt to be overwhelmed. One looks instinctively for the words " Medaillé " in one corner and " don de l'Etat " in the other. The attitude of the nude youth who stands at the edge of the wood gazing at the sea and flapping his hands " To the Morning Sun " is more idiotic than is usual with this painter. Near the Tuke hangs a superficially-attractive picture by Nevin du Mont, of a Spanish girl, " Ni mas ni menos," with the conventional red rose in hair and hand on hip. On the same wall is an efficient and (dare I say it?) rather " oil-cloth-ish " picture of a Scottish country house by D. Y. Cameron. The greens are hard, vivid, well-varnished; the end of a white house shows itself in the middle of the picture in a setting of autumnal foliage, and there are some figures here and there on the drive leading up to the house. I much preferred Wilson Steer's tranquil, mysterious and imaginative landscape, " Ironbridge Salop," which hangs in another part of the room. With the possible exception of one which I fancy belongs to Mr. W. S. Maugham, this is the best Steer I have ever seen. Charles Shannon's circular picture, " A Bunch of Grapes," in achieving a certain sensuous decorative quality, only just escapes the pretty-pretty. Mrs. Swynnerton's " The

Young Mother" was, I must confess, a disappointment. The young peasant woman holding her baby in her arms stands against a background of apple trees loaded with fruit, and through the trellis-work of branches can be seen a bay with a headland in the distance. The picture, naturally enough, considering the skilled hand which painted it, has many beauties, but much of my personal enjoyment of it was spoilt by the expression on the mother's face. She is the "art" peasant, as conceived by city-dwellers, to the life, and her whole appearance is steeped in that factitious "wistfulness" which is such a deadly enemy of all true art. Wilson Steer's "The Blue Girl," which hangs opposite Mrs. Swynnerton's picture, shows the great landscape painter in his less attractive Chelsea mood. In a corner of the room hangs "The Finding of Moses," by that difficult, original, rather baffling genius, Simeon Solomon; and hanging above the marble chimney-piece is a big, bold "Venus and Mars" by Brangwyn. This picture, like so many of Brangwyn's paintings, seems to give the spectator a hearty slap on the back. To look at it is like being blown upon by a boisterous wind. Other pictures which I remember in this room are a small study of a child by Frank Potter, which hangs on a screen; and rather a poor example of the art of Sir

W. Q. Orchardson, that fine but mis-appreciated genius.

On the staircase leading to the second floor, the "Harrowing" of a purple field by Léon Little is balanced on the opposite wall by a picture of Norman Garstin's called "The Stranger," which bears the hated word "Newlyn" in one corner. The hanging of these two works is eminently tactful—one of the many instances of the fine discrimination with which the collection has been arranged.

The collection of drawings and water-colours hung in the front rooms on the second floor is full of interest and well repays the climb. It is particularly rich in examples of the art of that robust genius Hercules Brabazon. There are also a number of water-colour drawings by Charles Conder and by Simeon Solomon; at least seven examples of Constantine Guys' vivid transcripts from the social life of his day; and characteristic drawings by John, Orpen, and W. Rothenstein. In a little closet which serves as the print room are the originals of one or two of Max Beerbohm's most famous caricatures, including Mr. George Moore's "Introduction (by W. B. Yeats) to the Queen of the Fairies." There is now one more room to be explored—a small square apartment at the back of the house, from whose windows one has almost as wide a view over the roofs of Dublin as one gets of the red roofs of Brussels from the water-colour room in the Musée Moderne. The gem of this little room, to my mind, is Conder's "Stormy Day, Brighton," which shows this artist in a less familiar but more finely-inspired mood than do his "Fêtes Galantes." "The Gondoliers," by Conder, which hangs near by is a fair example of his more usual manner, and it is interesting to compare the two.

As one returns through the various rooms of the gallery, stopping again in each before the things which interest one most—in one room Guys' "Entry of Queen Isabella" in sepia, and Brabazon's marvellous "Tangier;" in another, John's "Portrait Study" and Steer's lovely "Ironbridge, Salop" one is struck by the wide range of the collection and by the wonderful taste and skill with which the pictures have been classified and hung. With the exception of the Constables there are perhaps no pictures of really first-rate excellence (pending the return of the masterpieces constituting Sir Hugh Lane's "Conditional Gift"); but, on the other hand, there is scarcely any rubbish, scarcely anything which does not possess interest or significance of one kind or another. And of how many public collections in the whole world can this be said? When the new gallery has been built, and the Lane treasures restored to the collection for which their owner acquired them, Dublin will possess a gallery of modern art second to none in Europe save the Luxembourg, a gallery which in the years to come, when Ireland once again has a Parliament of her own, will do much to add to its importance as a capital city.

CHAPTER VII.

The National Portrait Gallery.

The quality of charm which seems such an evanescent thing that it must die with the individual who possesses it, has in reality a strange vitality. Unlike other good qualities, it cannot be "interred with the bones" of those who display it. The dullest of histories cannot obscure it; those who throughout the ages have been remarkable for it, even if they never accomplished anything memorable, have an unwarrantable tendency to be remembered. Even the most biassed of chroniclers can rarely succeed in robbing an historical character of his charm though he may rob him of everything else, and paint his moral character in the blackest hues. It makes no matter, for example, what historians may tell us of the perfidy of King Charles II. His charm eludes them all and survives as successfully as the charm of Charles Lamb, of Nell Gwynne, of Lord Edward Fitzgerald, Dr. Johnson, Oliver Goldsmith, and a hundred more who might as easily be named. And how many women there are who continue making conquests through the centuries—long after their lovely flesh has rotted from their bones! Charm is undying. Men will rise up to fight in defence of Mary Queen of Scots in the generations to come as chivalrously as they fought for her four centuries ago. And always men will go on regretting that it does not fall to everyone's lot to go to Corinth. Yet who was Lais but a mere courtesan? She has not even left us, like Sappho, a few golden fragments of song.

The National Portrait Gallery in London—a series of cavernous rooms filled with portraits of people who during their lives raised by their own exertions, imperishable monuments to their fame—is, to my mind at all events, a place to avoid. Yet it contains many rare works of art, and most of the faces which meet one's eyes on its walls are those of men and women who in their lifetimes accomplished much, and whose careers were full of historical interest. The Dublin "National Portrait Gallery," on the contrary, contains among its portraits the counterfeit presentment of only a few individuals who seem to have accomplished anything, of only a handful of painters, poets, novelists or statesmen who can even charitably be described as more than second-rate. And yet, so far from being a place to avoid, it is so attractive as to be positively exciting. Immediately the visitor finds himself in interesting company. All the

Irish great seem to have been men who were spendthrift of their personalities, giving most generously to the social life of their time all that they possessed of wit, of creative energy, intelligence, fantasy, or charm. They did not hoard their gifts as is the English habit, laying down their wit in great books as one lays down wine in the cellar. They poured out everything they had recklessly, to immortalise the moment, receiving from their contemporaries that immediate recognition which is the reward of the actor or the singer, and leaving to posterity only the lingering fragrance of their charm to make them memorable. For this reason to walk through the rooms of the National Portrait Gallery in Dublin is like spending a morning in the very best of company. The experience is amusing and stimulating: anything but dull.

The rooms of the National Portrait Gallery are arranged according to dates, the one nearest the entrance containing the most modern portraits. On the way into this first (or last) room, the large picture by Francis Wheatley of "A Review of Troops in the Phœnix Park by Gen. Sir John Irwin," which hangs in the passage outside it, should not be passed unnoticed. Wheatley's merits as a painter seem scarcely to be recognised adequately; and the present picture, though not one of his best, has many attractive qualities.

Generally speaking, the latest generations of the Irish great seem hardly to have reached the same level of interest as their immediate predecessors. One of the most arresting of the nineteenth century portraits is the boldly-painted self-portrait by the elder Catterson Smith. Here this most unequal painter is seen at his best; he is painting now to please himself, not as a tradesman anxious to give " satisfaction " to a titled customer, but as an artist pure and simple. He has allowed some of that arrogance which (however much it may be smothered) is part of nearly every artist's make-up, to show itself. The face is full of pride, the face of a sarcastic, dignified, yet rather weak man, a man at war with himself perhaps. It is interesting to contrast this picture with the highly-finished but lifeless portrait of the fourth Earl of Bessborough, by the same hand, which hangs near by. There is no sincerity in the painting of the face, and the artist has used his brains merely to enable him to see the Earl as the Earl might like to see himself. The rendering of the fabrics of the Earl's robes, however, the painting of the linen, the black velvet, the ermine, the ribbon and jewel of the Order of St. Patrick, has been done with real interest on the part of the artist, who, like many craftsmen before him, seems to have revelled in his own dexterity. But the portrait shows none of the painter's higher qualities or potentialities. Perhaps the best picture by Catterson Smith which is exhibited in Dublin is the portrait of the Hon. Mrs. Latouche, of Bellevue, which hangs elsewhere, in the National Gallery. The painting of Mrs. Latouche's hands is masterly; and the shadowy, "suggested" room in which she is sitting with her left arm resting on a table, has been rendered with rare success. There are in this picture all the accessories for a portrait of first-rate excellence. But, alas, when it came to the painting of the face, the artist abdicated and made way for the tradesman.

Among the other noticeable modern portraits is a drawing of Mangan, the poet, made immediately after his death, in which one can read all the tragedy of that erratic, brilliant and tortured life. It is a relief to turn from it and look at the unfinished portrait of Maclise, done by himself when a boy of eighteen, which hangs near. This sketch shows the painter's gifts in a considerably more attractive light than do the huge subject pictures of which he subsequently became so fond. And yet, in the style which he affected, Maclise always was a good technician. No doubt his imagination was commonplace, but if he regarded painting purely as a craft, at least he made himself proficient in it. The portrait of himself, however, made for a friend, has a freshness and spontaneity which his later work missed. And what a charming face it is, with the curly brown hair, full pouting lips and eager eyes! Almost equally attractive is the pencil sketch of Samuel Lover as a young man, done by himself, which hangs near by. Lover's appearance, as is the way with most of us, did not improve as he grew older; but from this early pencil sketch one can easily imagine how popular the versatile Irishman must have been in drawingrooms in Dublin and in London how warmly women must have cared for him. Another portrait of great charm, in the same room, is that of Captain Taylor, a patron of the arts who founded the Taylor Scholarships. The picture shows him in the scarlet uniform of his regiment, and he is irresistible with his warm dark eyes and finely-bred sensitive face. Lawrence's drawing of Richard, Marquess Wellesley, shows us a colder, more purely "aristocratic" type. It is a face characteristic of the old *régime* at its best—hard, distinguished and responsible.

Further on, hanging in a miniature case behind a green curtain, the curious will discover a little portrait of James Gandon, the English architect whose genius has done so much to beautify Dublin. He has a large, dome-like bald head, and is dressed in a great red coat trimmed with fur. This portrait is by Horace Hone, a better example of whose art is to be found in the miniature of himself which hangs in the same case. To my mind, the most arresting of the portraits in this room (Room IV.) is that of John Philpot Curran. I refer to the picture of him by an unknown painter. The one by Hugh Douglas Hamilton which hangs beneath it is lifeless, perfunctory and almost devoid of interest. The sitter's lips are agreeably parted, and one gets the impression that Hamilton, anticipating the bad photographer of modern times, has insisted that his subject should "look pleasant." There is nothing "pleasant" in the savage, unhappy, passionate yet not unlovable face which looks at one from the unknown's canvas. There is something almost ape-like about it. The long protruding lower lip, the blue upper lip, the almost triangular-shaped black eyebrows over dark eyes show us a personality which, whether for good or ill, was not ashamed to be itself. Mr. W. G. Strickland, who has been largely concerned with the forming of this collection, and to whose scholarship and taste it owes much, holds the view that this portrait is by James Petrie (father of the better known George Petrie, P.R.H.A.), who practised as a miniature painter in Dublin during the latter half of the eighteenth century. The painter must in any case have been a man of fearless honesty, a kind of George Washington among portrait painters. One feels instinctively that this was Curran. So powerfully did the portrait affect me that I remember, soon after I first saw it, I went straight away to the National Library in order to try to discover who Curran was. It appeared that he was one of the most famous, most fearless, and most eloquent advocates at the Irish Bar towards the end of the eighteenth century. Even notorious bullies like Lord Clonmell quailed before him. He was the father of Sarah Curran, Robert Emmet's fiancée. In 1780 he was living at 4 Ely Place, a modest house now used as offices. Later he removed to a house called The Priory, on the outskirts of Dublin, on the banks of the river Dodder, which was searched by the military for treasonable papers at the time of Emmet's arrest. Sir Jonah Barrington says of Curran in his " Personal Sketches " that " his person was mean and decrepit, very slight, very shapeless—with nothing of the gentleman about it; on the contrary, displaying spindle limbs, a shambling gait, one hand imperfect, and a face yellowed and furrowed, rather fat and thoroughly ordinary. . . But his rapid movements, his fire, his sparkling eye, the fine and varied intonations of his voice— these conspired to give life and energy to every company he mixed with." It is curious how any contemporary observer could have thought the face in Petrie's portrait " thoroughly ordinary." It is certainly one of the least " ordinary " that I have ever seen in any portrait that I can recall. Curran, we are told by the same authority, possessed great courage, personal and political, and fought many duels. " In private he was unfortunate and full of sores. His griefs, too, were frenzies. He had moments of rapture, but few of repose." "His talk " (says Crabb Robinson) " was rich in idiom and imagery and in warmth of feeling. He was all passion—fierce in his dislikes, and not sparing in the freedom of his language. . . ."

A little portrait of James Petrie, by himself, hangs close to what may perhaps be his masterpiece, and shows him to have been a shaggy and unkempt individual, in appearance suggesting an ostler—an honest, jovial, rather truculent, downright sort of man, and clearly no sycophant.

The Dublin Portrait Gallery has three interesting Hogarths—a portrait of Dr. Hoadley and two smaller portraits, one of General Wade, the other of the second Viscount Boyne. The pose of Viscount Boyne is very original and amusing, and the whole portrait is instinct with the personality of the artist if not of his subject. A more immediately attractive but less remarkable face than Curran's is that of Denis Daly, an M.P. in Grattan's Parliament, whose portrait in a canary-coloured flowered waistcoat was painted by Reynolds. The picture now in the Gallery is a contemporary copy of the original. It shows us a buoyant, reckless personality with all the recognised Irish characteristics. Just above him hangs Hamilton's portrait of the Hon. David Latouche, a gentleman with a large white face, heavy nose, double chin and a regard full of subtlety and intelligence in which the humorous and the sardonic appear to be equally blended. He looks like a "three-bottle" man, which no doubt he was. Among a group of eighteenth century Irish statesmen is a good portrait of the Earl of Charlemont dressed in the uniform of the Irish Volunteers, by William Cuming; and Gilbert Stuart's memorable picture of Henry Grattan. Grattan's face, in this portrait, is of a singular and arresting beauty. He has a long, slightly arched nose, thin lips, waving white hair and brown eyes full of vivacity and fire. But half the beauty of the face lies in its expression which eludes description, but which the painter has succeeded in rendering. Other interesting things in the same room are a painted wax bust of Francis, Lord Rawdon, afterwards Earl of Moira; and a portrait, by

C. Allingham, of Thomas Dermody, the poet, who looks as if the pursuit of the muse had given him a colic. Close to Dermody hangs a capable portrait of Barry, the painter, by John Opie.

In portraits of famous Irish beauties and "toasts" the gallery is fairly rich, but as is so often the way, most of them seem scarcely to do justice to the ladies' reputed comeliness. Kitty Monroe has been turned by Angelica Kauffmann into a good German woman, like a princess in some small German court. Kitty Clive, the actress, painted by Jonathan Richardson, does not look attractive; neither indeed does the stiff and starched Maria Gunning of Francis Cotes' portrait. Charles Jervas in his picture of Stella has given the poor lady gumboils; but in the other portrait of her painted by an unknown artist, it is possible to realise in looking at this girl with pretty neck and shoulders rising out of a bodice of peacock-blue, with warm brown eyes and hair, piquant nose and well-poised head, what it was that Swift saw in her. A picture of Peg Woffington, by John Lewis, which hangs on the same wall is at first attractive, then not, then attractive again. The actress wears a very pretty grey hat with grey streamers, and a grey dress edged with lace. But her face is large, and at the second glance seems strangely vapid with its long oval eyes set wide apart under a narrow forehead. But gradually the picture begins once again to charm. There is a "something" there which the artist, perhaps in spite of himself (for he seems to have been but a mediocre portrait-painter), has succeeded in seizing and rendering. Other interesting portraits of players are Ozias Humphrey's charming pastel of Eliza Farren, and Gainsborough's large full-length portrait of James Quin.

From the point of view of æsthetic rather than historic interest, I think among the things which gave me most pleasure in the Portrait Gallery were Robert Healy's chalk drawings of himself and of his brother William. Who Robert Healy might be I did not know, for I never heard of him before. The drawings appear to be done partly in chalk, partly in sepia, and look as if they were the work of some art student with a touch of genius. The two self-portraits are dated 1765 and 1766 respectively, and the later one is perhaps the more successful. The artist has one hand resting on a cast of some classical head from which he has probably been working; in the other hand is a crayon, and he is looking up in the middle of his work with parted lips and eyes wide open and eager. One of the qualities which (to my mind at all events) lifts this drawing out of the commonplace is the fact that it has an *idea* at the back of it. It is the result of a definite, and most happy, conception in the artist's brain. The portrait is fresh, vivid, informal, strangely alive, full of fun and of a kind of ecstacy of youthfulness and high spirits—in short, a naïf revelation of personality. Even the plaster cast has a vitality of its own. The work of these two brothers interested me so much that I took the first opportunity of finding out the little that appears to be known about them. The following is the most salient part of the entry relating to them in Mr. Strickland's "Dictionary of Irish Artists":—

Healy (or Haly), Robert (ff. 1765—1771).

Portrait and animal painter in chalks. Trained in the Dublin Society's schools, he established himself as an artist in Wood Quay, and from there exhibited portrait drawings at the Society of Artists in William Street in 1766 and 1767. In 1768 he was in Essex Quay, and in 1769 and 1770 at No. 2 Dame Street. He exhibited in each of these years portraits in water-colour and in chalk, and in 1770 was awarded a silver palette by the Dublin Society for the best exhibited drawing of a group of figures. Healy enjoyed a considerable practice and had a high reputation for his portraits, both of men and horses, drawn in black and white chalk. His work is effective, though his figures are somewhat stiff; but his portrayal of horses, which was considered his chief excellence, is poor. A number of his drawings, chiefly portraits of members of the Connolly family and their favourite horses, are at Castletown, Co. Kildare. They include " The Rt. Hon. Thomas Connolly and his wife, Lady Louisa Connolly," and " The Duke of Leinster and friend skating near Carton," both drawn in 1768. Three of his drawings belong to Lt.-Colonel Burgh at Oldtown, Co. Kildare: portraits of " Mrs. Gardiner," dated 1769, " Mrs. Cradock " and "Florinda Gardiner and her Nurse." Pasquin mentions a " Fox and Cock " done for Lord Mountjoy, as " much admired by all connoisseurs," and also says of his drawings, that they " are proverbial for their exquisite softness; they look like fine proofs of the most capital mezzotint engravings;" a not inapt description. . . ." Healy died in July, 1771, from the effects of a cold brought on while sketching cattle in Lord Mornington's park. The " Hibernian Magazine," in noticing his death, refers to him as " a gentleman of an excellent taste and original genius in his profession." Mr. Strickland refers to the work of the younger Healy (William) as being almost indistinguishable in style from that of his brother. It seems clear from these quotations that Robert Healy's work was highly thought of by the connoisseurs of his day, and their judgment is not to be despised.

One of the few pictures by foreign artists in the National Portrait Gallery is a portrait, ascribed to Pietro Longhi, of General Christopher Nugent. Nugent was a soldier of fortune who presumably made a career for himself in Venice in the days when the Venetian Republic was dancing, drinking, gambling and flirting itself into its grave. The portrait is painted with great care for minutiæ, and gives an effect of brilliance. The General stands in the "first position," by a table on which lies a map of England. With his right hand he points to where London is marked; in the left he holds his hat and stick. He is elegantly dressed in a blue coat, buff-coloured waistcoat and black knee-breeches. The pose, however, is almost grotesquely formal: and competent and highly-finished as the portrait is, it has nothing of the higher qualities either of portraiture or picture-making. It is lifeless and empty and shows no trace of the intense personal interest and humour with which Pietro Longhi has infused his carnival scenes in the London National Gallery. I was not surprised to discover later that the attribution is incorrect and that the portrait is not by Pietro but by Alessandro Longhi.

In the remaining room, which has not yet been touched on, are hung the earliest of the portraits, those dating from the sixteenth and seventeenth centuries. The two pictures, one of Queen Mary and the other of Queen Elizabeth, of the school of Lucas de Heere; Kneller's splendid "Baron de Ginkell," one of the best examples of his work in any public gallery; and the two little portraits wrongly attributed to Lely—one in pastel of the first Duke of Ormonde, the other, in water colour and chalk of Mary of Modena—are perhaps the most interesting of its contents. The Kneller portrait was a revelation to me, and I have never before seen such a fine example of this rather unsympathetic painter's art. The face is painted with great freedom and vigour and the background which shows a town in flames (Athlone perhaps) and troops fording a river through the smoke, is admirably done. The whole picture is full of spirit and is much the best of the five portraits by this artist which the gallery possesses.

Supplementary to the portrait gallery proper are two print rooms, the larger of which houses an extensive collection of mezzotint portraits of Irish celebrities. The smaller print room contains a number of views of Dublin and its neighbourhood, of which the most interesting are a series of water-colour drawings of architectural subjects relieved by figures, by James Malton, the engraver.

However slowly I go through a picture gallery I always like before leaving it to hurry once again through the rooms, reviving pleasant memories. And small as it is, the Dublin National Portrait Gallery seems always to hold some fresh interest that was missed on the previous journey. It is a delightful place to walk through quite casually. To be in it is like finding oneself in an assembly of people whose names a companion mentions sometimes with a word or two of comment, sometimes without. Instinctively one picks out the interesting faces, those which seem most richly endowed with personality or character; and " thank the Lord " one exclaims, " no one here '*does* things.' " One feels that for the most part these people are content to move elegantly in the society in which they find themselves. If they wrote poems and so on it was either the pretty trifling of the amateur, or else it was done for the moment, to give a passing pleasure. The frumpiness which sometimes goes with natural genius, but more often with that tedious capacity for taking pains which sometimes produces a colourable imitation of genius, is hardly to be noticed in any of these witty, expressive faces unless it be in the florid countenance of William Carleton. But then of Carleton I have read somewhere that in private life he was "not distinguished by any of the humour which appears in his writings. His conversation "—says the same contemporary—" is generally of a thoughtful and melancholy cast and, unless when he is excited, distinguished by no very remarkable quality." So that Carleton does not seem to have been a typical Irishman. Or perhaps it is merely that unlike most of the company in which he finds himself in the National Portrait Gallery, he was not out of the gentry, but was the son of a small farmer in County Tyrone, getting his education at a hedge school and coming to Dublin as a boy with only coppers in his pocket, to try his luck—inspired to such an adventure by having read " Gil Blas " !

No doubt it was Carleton's creative faculties—I am presuming that he possessed them, for I never read him—which make him seem different from the personalities who surround him. For to any visitor who walks quickly through these rooms it must, I think, seem apparent that the normal Irishman is rarely creative and invariably dramatic and expressive, rich in personality, in wit, in social gifts. How many orators there are, how many duellists, patriots, rebels, actors and how many, how very many charming people of both sexes of whom nothing except their personal attractiveness is still remembered ! Thomas Moore is an example of a man whose personal charm lives on undiminished. He has managed to weld it into his apparently worthless " Irish melodies " to such an extent that they have

THE PORTRAIT GALLERY 143

triumphantly survived one century and will probably survive another.

> Oft in the stilly night
> Ere slumber's chain hath bound me,
> Fond mem'ry brings the light
> Of other days around me—

Turn it upside down, look at it from every angle, it makes no matter. You can find nothing in it. But something there is: it has charm. What is this " charm," when all is said? Is it better to be charming or to be creative? Which is the higher type, the artist—often in private life a mere squeezed orange of a man if he have genius—or the appreciator for whom, even if unconsciously, the artist works? I cannot even attempt to answer these riddles. It has been said of charm that "it is the quality which enables us to get more for our goods than they are worth." When we call the Irish " charming," are we in truth making a just if bitter criticism of the Irish character? Again, the question is much too profound for me to attempt to tackle. Besides, I know too well that I, in any case, am one of charm's readiest victims. Charm is the quality, the weapon, which of all others I find myself least able to resist.

One omission I have noticed in the Dublin National Portrait Gallery. It contains, as yet, no portrait of Sir Hugh Lane; and one cannot but wonder whether sooner or later the Sargent picture will ever find its way here. In the personality of Sir Hugh Lane, so far as one who never knew him can recreate it from the testimony of his friends, there seems to have been blended energy, discrimination and a rare capacity to accomplish—together with all the charm you please. The presence of his portrait would add the final touch of completeness to that conspectus of the Irish character which the gallery affords.

CHAPTER VIII.

The National Gallery of Ireland.

The National Gallery in Leinster Lawn is a curiously grim place compared with the Harcourt Street Gallery. It seems anxious to guard its treasures for the attendants who—tastefully disposed about its empty rooms—doze peacefully on their chairs. It greets the chance visitor with a freezing silence, making him feel as if he had penetrated into some great house of which the owner, whilst holding himself unable to refuse admittance, does not feel called upon to encourage enthusiasm or to extend a welcome. At first one misses the cosmopolitan cheeriness of continental galleries, but if one perseveres the chill wears off, the frigidity melts and after a time a delightful feeling of intimacy takes its place. Perhaps even picture galleries are susceptible to admiration.

Admiration of a most ungrudging kind will certainly be called forth from all lovers of painting who visit the Dublin National Gallery. The collection is large and important, probably the most important of its kind in the British Isles outside the

London National Gallery. It consists of about 560 pictures, 600 original drawings, water colours, &c.; 570 engraved portraits, and a number of busts and statues in bronze and marble, together with a collection of casts from the antique for the use of students. It possesses several works of the first importance, including a Mantegna and an incomparable El Greco, and a unique collection of Dutch pictures, while a feature of the gallery is the number of masterpieces it contains by comparatively little known painters. In order to gain a thorough knowledge of all its treasures many months of study would be necessary, and writing now from a distance I can only speak of those pictures which remain most clearly in my memory. Of them all I think the one which has impressed me most is El Greco's "Vision of St. Francis." This marvellous painting, with its cold blues and stone greys takes one at once into an esoteric religious atmosphere. It is in every sense of the word inspired. The desire of all who follow a religion, no matter of what kind the religion may be, is by a life of holiness to obtain a measure of understanding of Divine things. In El Greco's Ecstacy of St. Francis, this mystic with genius shows us the religious life with all its agonies and all its spiritual compensations, shows us the hunger of the human soul for God. The picture is one

THE NATIONAL GALLERY

of sheer beauty of the highest and most difficult kind. The impression which it made on me when I first saw it in London some years ago, has only been increased by constant visits to it in Dublin. It is a picture of which it is impossible to tire, for everything which really "matters"— whether we realise it or not—is contained in it. On its frame one notices with gratitude the familiar words, "presented by Sir Hugh Lane," and looking at the indifferent examples of Spanish art by which it is surrounded, one's gratitude is increased. What an enormous advantage it is to a gallery to be under the direction of a real connoisseur, of an enthusiast with knowledge! Every picture which Sir Hugh Lane presented fills a gap. He did not fill up all the gaps, for he did not live long enough, but all his gifts had a point. There was an idea behind them. One feels that they were just the pictures needed by the rooms to which they were added. For example, without the Greco the Spanish room would have been poor indeed. It contains a curious picture by Morales of St. Jerome in the Wilderness—very different, with its sombre scheme of browns, from those Madonnas "with high, egg-shaped foreheads" which Aubrey Beardsley so much admired—which remains in the memory, and two rather indifferent Goyas of which the portrait of the Conde del Tajo is the better. But lovers of Goya would prefer to see him not represented at all than represented by these examples.

After the Greco, I think the picture which gave me most delight was the splendid Mantegna in the big central room where the Italian pictures are hung. In regard to Italian art I must confess shamelessly to several heresies. The interest of some of the early Italian masters, whose works fetch (for the moment) such inflated prices, seems to me to be purely that which attaches to "antiques." For American millionaires the merely antique has no doubt an overpowering charm. Unfortunately, their purchases push up prices and thereby impress the trustees of public galleries who, in consequence, not infrequently squander large sums of public money on tedious "primitives." For those who care little for the sums which pictures may be worth in cash, and everything for the actual delight they give to their possessors, a collection of pictorial curios even though they are Italian, has very little æsthetic significance. Such pictures tend to turn a picture gallery into a museum, and to overwhelm such real masterpieces of Italian art as the Dublin Mantegna. Luckily the Italian room in the Dublin National Gallery, though to my mind it contains a number of dull, second-rate works, is fairly free from mere "curios."

The Mantegna, however, stands out resplendent in its glory. The picture is painted in tempera and the subject is " Judith with the Head of Holofernes." It is in grisaille, with flecks of colour on the side of the tent. Exquisite in composition, it has an almost startling vitality and sincerity. The folds of Judith's dress, her attitude and expression as she holds the severed head of Holofernes ready to drop it into the bag held open for her by the attendant negress, can never be forgotten by anyone who has seen the picture. Mr. Bernard Berenson the great authority on Mantegna, has justly described the Dublin Judith as " one of the masterpieces of Italian art, as composition, as arrangement, as modelling, as movement to be surpassed only by Mantegna himself."

There is certainly vitality and a kind of archaic charm in Fra Angelico's curious " Attempted Martyrdom of Saints Cosmus and Damianus." The colour and arrangement are pleasing; it is a herald of the dawn; but considered purely as a work of art without regard to its date or to the prestige of the painter's name I cannot see that it is in anyway comparable with the Mantegna. To my mind it does not gain anything æsthetically from the fact that it is naïf. I cannot see that naïveté in a work of art is necessarily a virtue any more than age or " authenticity " are virtues.

(No one but a snob or a pedant would covet a picture merely because it was authentic.)

After the " Judith " one of the things in the Italian room which I remember with most pleasure is the " Portrait of a Musician," ascribed to Botticelli. The picture is painted on a panel, in tempera. At first glance I got the impression that the background must have been painted in later than the head; and I was a little taken aback when I saw the ascription. However, these questions of scholarship are too high for me. Whether the portrait is by Botticelli or by some other master, it is certainly a picture of the greatest interest. The " Story of Lucretia," on the other hand, though it seems in many ways more characteristic of Botticelli, is clearly an inferior work and will scarcely give an Irish student a just idea of this great master.

Of the three Veroneses—two from the Milltown collection, " The Finding of Moses " and " Europa and the Bull," and a large " Portrait of a Lady " presented by Sir Hugh Lane—the one I liked best was " The Finding of Moses." For all I know (or care) it may not be a Veronese at all, but it struck me as a work full of charm which any gallery would be proud to possess. Pharaoh's daughter, very ladylike and sumptuously dressed and reminding one for all the world of the manageress of a fashionable boarding house, looks down

THE NATIONAL GALLERY 151

at the naked foundling which is being held up for her inspection. There is a wood at her back, and to the left a river, crossed by a bridge, with the spires of a city in the distance. In the foreground, a nigger with glittering eyes and teeth bends forward in excitement, and behind him a girl in a beautifully painted white frock is turning her back on the scene and bending down to scratch the sole of her foot. The picture is a little gem, and I have returned to it again and again and like it better every time. The "Portrait of a Lady," in her elaborate orange dress embroidered with gold and seed pearls, with her fat, ringed hands and thin-lipped spiteful face, commands respect, partieularly for the shape and poise of the head, but is scarcely enticing.

There are a good many pictures in this room, including Francia's "Lucretia," and Guercino's perfectly odious "St. Joseph with the Holy Child" and others which need not be specified, which to me were tedious in a way which no Dutch or German picture of the same periods could possibly equal. The few good pictures by late Italians—for example the landscape by Magnasco, a Genoese who died in 1747; the grandiose landscape by the now despised Salvator Rosa; and Guido Reni's masterly "Group of Saints interceding for the City of Bologna"—shine out from among numerous indifferent canvases whose sole merit seems to be that they were produced in a more glorious epoch. The Guido Reni pleased me particularly, and I think I never saw a better example of his corrupt talent. How bored and languid looks the Virgin as she sits enthroned on a cloud in her exquisitely-painted red and blue robes. She glances down at the upturned faces of the deputation of eminent saints who are beseeching her to have pity on plague-stricken Bologna. Little angels, like cupids, float round her on either side, ready to drop roses on to the heads of the suppliant ecclesiastics when the signal shall be given. But alas, to-day there is " nothing doing ": Our Lady is in a difficult mood. She will never give that signal: the roses will not fall. Saints Francis of Assisi, Dominic, Charles Borromeo, Francis Xavier, George and Petronius (I like Petronius) may plead with all the dignified persistence at their command, but she declines to hear them. Meanwhile the city can be seen far away below her, under a black cloud, and the bodies of the dead are being hurried from its gates by the terrified inhabitants. It is really too bad of her! For sheer brilliance of technique combined with an entire absence of any sort of religious feeling, this picture would be difficult to surpass. It has a rare flavour of depravity and cynicism which the eighteen-nineties never approached at their most daring.

Lest I should seem too unappreciative of the Dublin " old masters " I must mention two other pictures in this room which I remember very clearly—Mazzolini's whirling " Pharaoh and his hosts overwhelmed in the Red Sea " which rivets attention by its almost frenzied vitality and brilliance; and a very beautiful and tender " Holy Family " of the school of Ghirlandaio. The latter picture seemed to me one of the most appealing in the whole room, full of sincerity and religious feeling and in colour and arrangement most lovely.

But, on the whole, the Italian room in the Dublin National Gallery was I must own a disappointment to me. I have enough veneration for such masters as Botticelli, Titian, and Carpaccio to hate to see them unfairly represented. Is it not curious with what veneration really poor Italian pictures (even with illustrious names upon their frames) are still regarded? Anything really Italian, really " quatrocento " or " cinquecento " is generally considered sacrosanct. But if pictorial art reached its highest level in Italy during the time of the Renaissance—which few will contest—it was capable almost simultaneously of sinking fairly low. And nothing is more cloying to the taste, nothing more indigestible, than Italian painting of the second and third rank. Excellent as several of the Italian pictures in the Dublin collection undoubtedly are, and notwithstanding the superb Mantegna, it is really something of a relief to go from the large Italian room into the little room where the pictures by the German masters are hung. The change of atmosphere, almost one might say the change of "temperature" is in the highest degree refreshing. The German room has a keen, bracing air. The pictures on its walls are full of vigour and romance; and out of their strength comes a rare sweetness. They have the fragrance and savour of an older, simpler life. They are more pagan perhaps than most of the Italians, but (I am speaking, of course, only of the pictures in Dublin) they are often more sincere. I once, with astonishment, heard a very emphatic artist in a Dublin drawingroom assert that Germany had "never produced any painters!" I think if he went to Room XV. in the National Gallery of Ireland and studied the two pictures there by the "Master of the Holzenhausen Portraits," and the two by Wolfgang Huber he would come to a different conclusion. However spiteful one may feel at the moment against William and his enslaved horde of "Huns," it is surely rather a ridiculous proceeding to try to visit the sins of the children upon their remote ancestors.

THE NATIONAL GALLERY 155

Paintings by Wolfgang Huber, one of the most interesting of the early German masters represented in Dublin, are very rare, and the National Gallery is fortunate in possessing two such fine examples. The one I liked best was the portrait of Anthony Hundertpfundt. The subject is dressed in a loose garment of dull red with a great tippet of black fur, and he wears a flat dark cap on his head. The background is a wall relieved with an inscription on the left hand side bearing Hundertpfundt's name and the date 1526. Above the wall is a narrow stretch of blue sky—gay, enticing, flecked with small, white clouds. Herr Hundertpfundt is staring lugubriously in front of him, as if he were waiting in a prison yard on the morning of his execution.

There are two examples of the art of Lucas Cranach in this room, one of them a "Judith," the other a small picture of Christ on the Cross, with a view of Jerusalem in the background under a stormy sunset sky. The model for the Judith—a girl with slant eyes and low forehead: a singularly evil type—was evidently a favourite with Cranach for we meet her again and again in his compositions. Other memorable pictures in Room XV. (which scarcely contains anything which lacks interest), are the younger Pourbus' "Portrait of a Lady;" Holbein's much restored portrait of Sir Henry Wyatt; a Dirk Bouts', the vigour of which succeeds in overcoming its naïveté; a Gheerardt David panel of "Our Lord bidding farewell to his Mother;" and—perhaps most important of all—portraits of Katherina Knoblauchin and of her brother Heinrich Knoblauch, by the "Master of the Holzenhausen Portraits." There is something strangely romantic and fragrant about these last two pictures. Katherina is a handsome blonde girl of a familiar South German type. She is dressed in crimson with a richly-embroidered white underdress, and she wears a curiously-shaped cap embroidered with gold. Behind her we have a vista of a landscape which looks like a bird's eye view of fairyland with its enticing blue mountains, lakes and sunlit sky. Heinrich Knoblauch has on a flat, dark cap, and a dark brown "costume" and cloak opened to display a shirt wonderfully embroidered in gold. The background is rather similar to that in the companion portrait and just as alluring.

Among the works by Flemish masters which the gallery possesses are a remarkably fine Jordaens called "A Theological Allegory;" two pictures of saints—St. Francis receiving the stigmata, and St. Dominic—by Rubens, and also a composite picture called "Christ at the House of Mary," in which the figures are by Rubens, the landscape background by Breughel, and

THE NATIONAL GALLERY 157

the birds, fruit and other "accessories" by Jan van Kessel. The whole effect of this joint production is most happy and pleasing, and does the highest credit to the "firm."

One could spend a great deal of time very profitably in the early German and Flemish rooms, and as for the three Dutch rooms, months of study could be devoted to them alone. The Dutch rooms form perhaps the most noteworthy feature of the whole gallery. One of the first directors appears with great judgment to have purchased Dutch pictures at a time when they were "going" comparatively cheap. The tradition has been maintained by his successors, with the result that Dublin is endowed with treasures which, from the purely commercial point of view, must now be worth many times the sums originally paid for them. In these three rooms, which contain an exceptionally large number of canvases considering the wall space, there is hardly a single picture which is lacking in interest. The greatest names are not largely represented, but the gallery is rich in really fine examples by the less-known masters. Even, therefore, to those who are already fairly familiar with Dutch art, the rooms will afford many revelations and surprises. For example, the illustrious Jakob Ruisdael, with whose landscapes most people are conversant, is poorly represented here. On the other hand, his uncle Solomon, who is apt to be depreciated unduly, is represented by one of his finest works, a picture called "The Halt," which will cause many people to revise their ideas of him. It would be possible to go on multiplying instances of this kind, but the subject is too big to attempt in a short chapter. One of the few pictures which I regretted was the solitary Albert Cuyp, a poor and very misleading example, lacking in almost all the master's characteristic beauties. There are four Rembrandts, one of which, a little picture called "La Main Chaude" belonging to his early Leyden manner is a veritable gem. The other three are a dull "Head of a Young Man," a "Head of an Old Man," and a beautiful "Shepherds Reposing at Night." Among the many Dutch masters of whom the gallery contains first-rate examples are Beerstratin, Cornelis Troost, Pieter Codde, Cornelis Huysmans, Jan de Cappelle, Bega, Melchior d' Hondcoeter, the younger Van de Velde, Antoine Goubau, Jan Van Huysum and Paul Potter. It is difficult to pick and choose among such a collection, but I think two of the pictures in these rooms which have given me most pleasure are Paul Potter's "Head of a young White Bull with a wreath of flowers round his neck;" and Jan Van

Huysum's marvellous " Bouquet of Flowers." But as soon as the words are written a dozen others occur to one's mind.

The policy of acquiring the best works of the smaller masters has been carried out also with great success in the British rooms, where many surprises await the lover of painting. The gallery possesses admirable pictures by such men as Benjamin West, Julius Cæsar Ibbetson, Barker of Bath, J. Holland and Philip Reinagle—painters whose names, I must confess, conveyed little or nothing to me before I came to Dublin. Reinagle seems to have been one of those artist-craftsmen from whom, in the Age of Taste, one might have ordered a picture as one would a chest of drawers. The Congreve family appears to have done this, and the resulting picture of " Lady Congreve and her Children " must have given as much satisfaction to those who commissioned it as it affords us to-day. The little family group is posed rather stiffly in the foreground of an eighteenth century living-room which has been rendered by the painter with great minutiæ of detail. Every flower in the pattern of the beautiful carpet, and every picture on the walls is reproduced with extraordinary pains and fidelity, while the general effect of the painting is admirably decorative and pleasing. The same qualities are shown in an even higher degree in Benjamin Wilson's masterpiece, "Portraits of Mr. and Mrs. Richardson." The greens which are the key-note of this picture are exquisite. The couple stand in front of a little classical pavilion in a green, park-like garden. Mr. Richardson wears a green coat and breeches; his wife, who leans her arm affectionately on his shoulder, is dressed in grey silk with a black silk shawl round her shoulders. Two dogs, a Spitz and an Italian greyhound, appear in the foreground of the picture, the " finish " of which is simply dazzling in its perfection. It is not great art, perhaps, but of its kind, how exquisite!

Reynolds, Romney, Hogarth, Raeburn, Gainsborough, Hoppner, Richard Wilson, Wheatley are all represented more or less adequately. Hoppner, whom I had always hitherto regarded as a much over-rated painter is represented by a self-portrait most original in conception and most happy in its decorative effect: the best thing by him I ever saw. (Again we read, "Presented by Sir Hugh Lane.) On the other hand, any doubts which previously I may have entertained in secret about Romney were confirmed by the Dublin examples. His portrait of Mary Tighe shows him in his most languishing mood, while the "Titania, Puck and the Changeling" with the fair Emma as the model for

Titania has a winsomness that is positively sickly. The four oil paintings by Turner are none of them important, but the gallery is fortunate in possessing a fine set of Turner water-colours which are wisely displayed only for one month in the year, so that the freshness of their colouring is not endangered. Of the Gainsboroughs I must confess to a great liking for a small early landscape called " A view in Suffolk," in which Dutch influence is very noticeable. It is an enchanting picture, painted purely " for love."

Of the modern pictures of the British school, curiously enough by far the most attractive are Millais' large and joyous " Hearts are Trumps " and Landseer's unfinished portrait group of " Charles Kinnaird Sheridan, with his wife and child," painted in Paris in 1847. Millais' picture, which shows us three graceful English girls dressed in crinolines and playing cards in a mid-Victorian drawingroom, has even now a rare fragrance, and it is easy to imagine how it will be prized a century hence. The Landseer, which hangs near by, is the most astonishing thing by this painter that I have ever seen. Evidently, while he was painting this delightful work, which may perhaps have been inspired by friendship, he had momentarily forgotten what his public expected of him. Sheridan lies on a sofa with a little King Charles spaniel at his feet, and through the open window there is a view of the Seine. The prevailing tones of the picture are mauve and grey, and it is easy to believe that much of its beauty is due to the fact that mercifully it was left unfinished. A fine nude by Etty attracts attention among the British moderns, and the rooms contain also a landscape by Nathaniel Hone, and two pictures by Mulready which in spite of their superficial ugliness of colour, rather grow on one when they are examined closely.

The National Gallery is not particularly rich in French pictures, but there is a very fine Chardin in perfect preservation, called " Les Tours des Cartes "; a hard, brilliant Claude, " Juno confiding Io to the care of Argus;" several excellent Poussins; two " Groups of Dead Game," by Alexandre François Desportes, and a delicious " Mary Magdalene in the Desert " attributed to Jean Cousin.

The Venetian room is a little over-loaded by pictures from the Milltown collection, some of which, one feels, might advantageously be afforded a nice, dry home in the basement. A certain style is given to the room in which they hang by Piazzetta's bold but rather empty " Decorative Group "; but it would be greatly strengthened by the addition of a really good Guardi, or Tiepolo, or Pietro Longhi.

THE NATIONAL GALLERY

The large number of drawings in water-colour and black and white which form one of the most valuable features of the National Gallery are worthy of a great deal more attention than they usually receive. I have never encountered any other adventurous visitor beside myself in the water-colour rooms during the hours which I have spent in them, yet they form by no means the least interesting part of the whole collection. Here again, as in the Dutch rooms, it is difficult to know what to mention when there is so much that is good. There are drawings in red chalk by Watteau; a lovely Andrea del Sarto; a life-sized head in black chalk by Antonio del Pollajuolo; a " Head of a Girl " by Lorenzo di Credi; drawings in red chalk by Guercino and by Alfred Stevens; a very complete series of English water-colours by such men as David Cox, Copley Fielding, Callow and Sam Prout; a pretty gouache portrait of " Charles first Earl of Yarborough, as a boy," by Daniel Gardner; several small pastel portraits by H. D. Hamilton; and a large number of very interesting drawings by Dutch artists. Every visit to these rooms seems to yield a fresh " discovery." One day it may be Jurriaan Andriessen's curiously modern drawing in black chalk heightened by white, called " Visitors in a Studio "; another day Jan Both's three exquisite pen sketches, Rubens' drawing in pen and brown wash of "Susannah and the Elders," or perhaps Jacob Van der Ulft's "Entry of the Muscovite Embassy into Gorcum." But always one finds something fresh which one has not noticed before. I cannot imagine why these rooms should be so neglected, unless indeed Sir Frederick Burton's truly hideous "Venetian Lady"—which hangs on a screen near the entrance to the first of them—acts effectively as a deterrent.

One of the many interesting things about the Dublin National Gallery is the way in which succeeding directors have impressed it with their personalities. "Personality" in the making of a collection is a quality of obvious importance—as anyone may judge who takes the trouble to examine a list of the "bad" purchases made during the past generation by the Trustees of the London National Gallery. In Dublin the various directors seem to have had a fairly free hand. Some of them have made mistakes, but they cannot compare with the mistakes which have been made in Trafalgar Square. Such an idea as that of forming the collection of Dutch pictures at a time when these were easily obtainable can only have originated in a single brain. I do not know whose brain it was, but he certainly deserves a statue. As for Sir Hugh Lane, the touch of his transforming hand is seen in almost every room.

CHAPTER IX.

The Intellectuals.

When, on their appearance, I read Mr. George Moore's three volumes "Ave," "Salve," and "Vale," I remember feeling that, in spite of all the sly and malicious comments in them, they gave an extraordinarily attractive picture of his Dublin friends. It struck me at the time that he could scarcely have made it so attractive by any other method. We are never made to like people by hearing them cracked up by their intimates. Quite the contrary; the more intemperately they are praised the more we detest them in anticipation. The way to make people lovable is to laugh at them, to sneer at them possibly, but above all things to make them amusing. I arrived in Ireland, thanks to Mr. Moore's books, with the keenest interest in that circle of Dublin literary people which his genius (if not their own abilities) has probably rendered immortal. How he had invested them all with glamour: "dear Æ," John Eglinton, and the rest! There was a certain impish malice in some of the portraits, in those of Dr. Douglas Hyde, Sir Horace

Plunkett, Mr. T. P. Gill and even in that of W. B. Yeats; but all these people are big enough to render his treatment of them little more than a rather subtle compliment. I have never been able to sympathise with—or even quite to understand—the indignation expressed against Mr. Moore in certain circles. The wisest and most acute remark which I have heard in Dublin on the vexed question of Mr. Moore's indiscretions was made to me on one occasion by John Eglinton. "To make an appearance in one of George Moore's books," he observed, "is like having your portrait painted by a master. It is flattering, even though you may not personally be very pleased with the result."

I think there can be few more exciting experiences for a retiring person like myself—prone, in other people's houses, to creep into a corner and listen and look on—than a Dublin "literary evening." The atmosphere is at once novel and charming. There is much to observe. The uniformity of the London countenance—for the faces of Londoners are as much alike as the faces of London houses—is the first thing that one misses. A room full of Dublin people at once suggests the eighteenth century, for the glaze of the nineteenth was either never on them or it has been peeled off in the twentieth. The faces—interesting, odd, ugly, beautiful, vain, repulsive or alluring as they may be—are all astonishingly expressive. The electric lamp of personality which the Englishman is apt to switch off nervously when he finds himself in a crowd, in Dublin is turned on more brightly than ever as the crowd increases. I do not think that any Dublin intellectual ever feels really at ease in a *tête-à-tête* conversation, or with an audience of two. A Londoner of a similar type, on the other hand, will rarely unburden himself of any of his intimate ideas except in secret confabulation with a chosen friend.

No sooner has the stranger arrived at a Dublin " evening " and found his seat (after receiving a welcome which for its polished courtesy could scarcely be surpassed, even in France) than at once the stream of talk—interrupted momentarily by his arrival—flows on again all round him. And what talk! If there were any talk like this to be heard in London every golden word would be dished up in a volume of reminiscences and sold at 25s. net almost before the year was out. It is not chatter, it is not gossip; it is Conversation. Probably Mr. George Russell, large and shaggy-bearded, with dark grey eyes gazing through very strong glasses and fists raised to emphasise his point, will be heard by himself in a moment. But a sudden lull will never take him at a disadvantage. His theme will be perhaps " the importance of Co-operation in the National Life;" but, in any case, he will never be without a theme, for the capital letter subject seems to come to him as naturally as cooing to a dove. Never have I encountered any great man so verbally dexterous with gigantic questions, so easily profound. No wonder one tall young man sways like a lily above his head, sniffing in the words as they rise upwards, while two others of equal size, disposed on footstools, gaze from the floor in attitudes of veneration. There is, indeed, a great deal of the prophet about A. E., and the only thing which is disconcertingly out of the picture is the fact that he has so much honour in his own country.

When I first saw A. E. as it were enthroned with his satellites about him, for some reason which I cannot explain, my thoughts wandered away to a certain London tea-party which I attended in my youth. It was in the early days of a once famous literary review, with which I am very proud to have been in a humble way connected, and my editor had collected in his drawing-room some thirty or forty writers of varying degrees of importance. The lion cubs crowded together at the back of the room and roared shrilly among the teacups, abusing their publishers or denouncing one another. The chatter grew louder and louder, but I am certain that no one in the whole room broached a Subject, while if any-

THE INTELLECTUALS 169

one had attempted to formulate an Idea he would have been looked on as a conceited ass and rather underbred into the bargain. Now there was in this room a very great personage, one of the greatest living English writers and, as some think, one of the greatest novelists of all time. He was a little grey man, with grey eyes set wide apart, and he wore a red tie. He sat on an armchair next to an elderly lady of equally homespun appearance, and he seemed to be rather tired. At last there came a lull in the chatter—perhaps all the lion cubs were inspired to fill their jaws with pieces of cake at the same instant-minute. For a moment, in any case, the silence was complete, and through it, with electrifying effect, filtered the still, small voice of the father of English letters.

"And how is Tommy's whooping-cough?" he enquired, turning to his companion. . . .

I refuse to believe that any Irish literary celebrity would let down his admirers like this. Both Mr. Russell and Mr. W. B. Yeats would, I am sure, be incapable of it. On the two or three evenings in London, and now again in more homely surroundings in Dublin, when I have had a chance of listening to Mr. Yeats he has always said memorable things, and on a wide diversity of subjects. When I last saw him he remarked in passing, " there is no crime a nation will not commit if only its newspapers are wicked enough." But in addition to the capacity (which all fluent talkers possess) of crystallising current thought into a neat phrase, one feels when Mr. Yeats speaks that all the time his fine brain is working to its fullest capacity, at any moment that it may give forth some brilliant and illuminating flash on any subject which may happen to be under discussion. The connection between an Irishman's brain and his tongue appears to be far quicker and more certain than is the case with English people of equal mental calibre. Conversationally, the Irish never seem to lose their wits, and it follows from this that they have a formidable gift of repartee. Moreover, however, commonplace may be the opinions which they express, these opinions are delivered with such a clarity of phrasing and with such an astounding air of conviction that the dazzled visitor feels that the Oracle at last has spoken.

Among the subjects most frequently tackled conversationally in Dublin (besides " the condition of Ireland," that undying topic) are the War, the European situation, the future of the British Empire. To a stranger from London it is astonishingly attractive to hear such vast questions attacked so fluently and so well. It makes Dublin seem more than ever

THE INTELLECTUALS

like a foreign city with the additional advantage that one's own language is spoken in it. In London, as far as my own experience goes, most war talk or political talk resolves itself into the dreariest clichés, and is rarely attempted in the grand style except by half-pay colonels in the smoking rooms of political clubs. The London intellectuals usually content themselves with disjointed comments—occasionally suggestive, brilliant or startling—reserving any general conclusions at which they may arrive for privacy and their fountain pens. The great mass of English people do not, I believe, really think about the war at all, but content themselves with the easily assimilated catchwords with which their newspapers are full. Most of those who get as far as making an attempt to work things out for themselves find their thoughts at all points circumscribed by the bogey of "right feeling." If their thoughts look like carrying them in any direction of which they feel that the collective mind of the community (as expressed, of course, in the newspapers) would disapprove, they hastily suppress them. The effect of this mental timidity has been to cast England into the worst and most soul-destroying form of bondage which exists. No German invasion followed by the occupation of London and Liverpool, could possibly enslave us more than our own terrified unwillingness to follow out our own thoughts to their conclusions; our own shivering reluctance to surrender any of the cowardly prejudices which our newspapers unite to inflame. We mustn't ask what we are really fighting for, nor why our men should die to enable Russia to oust the Turk from Constantinople; we must continue to believe that every working man in the Central Empires is a double-dyed villain whom it is the duty of every other working man in the allied countries to surrender his liberties in order to exterminate. If we hear well-authenticated stories from our own returned soldiers that our foes are really much the same as other people, and quite capable of " heroism " (and even of magnanimity) we mustn't pay the least attention to them or modify in any way our desire " to crush." Such reason as we have left may insist on it: but " right feeling " makes it impossible.

In Dublin I have never detected the faintest trace of this mental constipation from which England is suffering, not even among the Unionists who believe heart and soul in the war. In Dublin one feels that men's thoughts are really *free*. I don't believe any Irishman could tolerate for an instant the kind of claptrap which in England does duty for opinions. Prejudices probably exist in Dublin, just as much as they do in London, but they are of a different nature and they are not so childishly absurd, nor so absolutely destructive of any and every form of ratiocination. To the Liberty-loving Englishman one of the most noticeable and pleasant things about Dublin is that it is a veritable stronghold of Liberty —perhaps one of the very few such strongholds left in Europe. From the shores of England our present and past Governments (despite their Liberal flavouring) have chased this lady, to the accompaniment of rotten eggs and all manner of abuse. Everything connected with her has gone, including even that right of Asylum for Russian political refugees and others, which for so many years has made England beloved by " oppressed nationalities " all over Europe. The descendants of the men who gave their lives in order to induce Liberty to abide with them have now turned round and kicked her out of doors. She has fallen down that well into which Militarism has already chucked the bayoneted bodies of Justice and Truth.

In Ireland the stranger feels that no such disaster could possibly befall the community. There freedom may be attacked from without, but it is not (as is the case with England) attacked from within. And freedom is surely more than anything a state of mind which can exist no matter to what outward forms of oppression the individual may be subjected. Remembering Lovelace's familiar platitude

("Stone walls do not a prison make") one may even hazard the guess that there is almost as much real liberty to be found inside Frongoch camp as in the whole of London. In a word, the calamity which seems to have befallen England is that not only has English liberty been sacrificed by its politicians, it has also been ejected from the hearts of the mass of individual Englishmen. In its place a press-controlled puppet labelled "patriotism" rears its lying and deceitful head. But in every Irish heart I imagine Liberty is now more venerated than she ever was before. I do not believe it possible that any Irish intellectual could allow his speculations, his conclusions, to be caged by anything except by the inevitable limitations of human mentality.

It was then this freedom of thought, particularly in the domain of world politics, this essential liberty, which struck me as the most valuable quality possessed by the Irish intellectuals whom I was fortunate enough to meet. I was far less impressed (save momentarily) by the talk I listened to about literature and the arts. The value of the opinions expressed on these and kindred topics seemed to be rarely on a level with the authority and brilliance with which they were delivered. When digested, much of what I heard about books and writers, the theatre and so on, struck me as being commonplace and narrow, and based on very imperfect knowledge. I have listened to an alleged littérateur giving a lengthy dissertation on Andreyef who (so it afterwards appeared) had never so much as heard of the "Sportsman's Sketches." And the very people who will talk to you in the most glowing terms about some poet who is either in the room or has just left it, will often follow it up almost immediately by some contemptuous reference to Irishmen like Bernard Shaw or George Moore, whose greatness all the English-speaking world acknowledges. I think I have never heard anywhere so much depreciatory nonsense talked about Mr. George Moore as I have heard in Dublin, or been in any literary circles where his books are so little read and so imperfectly appreciated. One of the largest circulating libraries in the city does not possess a single copy of "Esther Waters," of "Memoirs of my Dead Life," or of "The Lake." All the libraries, however, have many copies of "Ave," "Salve," and "Vale," and they are in constant request. A discussion about George Moore with a Dublin intellectual of either sex almost invariably resolves itself into a discussion of one or other of these three volumes. The effect of all this on anyone like myself who discovered in Mr. Moore one of the most sympathetic and æsthetically "tender" of modern writers before ever he gave a thought to the land of Mr. Moore's birth, was almost staggering. But if Mr. Moore is apt to be depreciated in Dublin, everyone continues to talk about him. How well he must have summed up the town (one feels) in the ten years of his stay there. And how cleverly, in the three volumes in which he has described those years, has he managed to find the deepest hiding-places of human vanity and to administer a tickling to his victims so exquisite as to be removed from pain only by a hair's breadth! I have seldom noticed the signs of a more intense and complex inward satisfaction than that displayed on the faces of those who tell one that they can "never forgive Mr. Moore" for one or other of his alleged iniquities, and I have met but few people in Dublin who seem able to keep George Moore the writer separate in their minds from that elderly gentleman with "champagne-bottle shoulders" who is occasionally to be noticed emerging from the Shelbourne Hotel.

It is a rough and ready token of critical sincerity when a man refuses to praise the work of some close friend which his critical faculty does not allow him to admire; it is a far more valuable sign of critical capacity and honesty of mind if credit is given to a writer's work when f r some reason or other his personality is distasteful to the critic. Miss Susan Mitchell, in her recent book on George Moore in the " Irishmen of the Day " series seems to me to have skilfully avoided both these tests. Her book is one of amusing personal anecdotes and is full of the humorous and occasionally bitter chidings of an attached friend. But throughout her study it is Mr. Moore the man rather than Mr. Moore the writer with whom she deals. Yet is it not in a man's lifework that the most important part of him, the most enduring part, is to be found? The world in this respect has always been charitable to its great men. History is more prone to record achievements than personal idiosyncracies, leaving the latter to be recorded chiefly by those scribblers of memoirs who write for idle women. There is a certain famous novelist who trumpets when he blows his nose and clears his throat in such a marked manner that his visitors are constrained to look nervously for the spittoon. But who will be so foolish as to think any the worse of his books for such a reason? The great have almost invariably their little absurdities, their little meannesses; and these are always particularly apparent to the feminine mind. Nevertheless, they are the great. I do not wish to suggest by all this that I am conversant with any of Mr. Moore's peculiarities whatever they may be: on the

M

contrary, he exists for me only in the pages of his books, many of which I admire. It was simply because I admire them so much that I found Miss Mitchell's study disappointing and was a little ashamed of myself for chuckling over it so gaily. Miss Mitchell certainly betrays the fact that she has read several of Mr. Moore's books; but she seems to have read them as one is sometimes apt to read a friend's works—without gusto and as a kind of social duty which cannot be avoided. Even when, as in the case of Esther Waters, she admires his work, she scarcely seems to conceal her fundamental lack of sympathy with the writer's point of view.

One of the charges I have heard made most frequently against Mr. Moore in Dublin is that of plagiarism, and I must confess the cases quoted have invariably left me unmoved. So long as the result achieved is successful it seems to me that an author of proved excellence should be at liberty, like a bird, to pick up straws wherever he will. The jackdaw propensities of a great writer seem to me to form but a poor peg on which to hang depreciation of his works. Depreciation, however—and depreciation of a particularly brilliant kind—has often struck me as being one of the characteristics of Dublin, just as a tendency to appreciate sometimes too readily and generously is one of the characteristics of London. Depreciation is a seductive art, one in which most writers are themselves adept, but I have seldom seen it brought to greater perfection than in Dublin. The diversion of crabbing the other fellows is generally preceded by a short religious ceremony. The depreciator first of all turns in the direction of Rathgar Avenue, he bows three times, he utters a short ejaculatory prayer in praise of A. E. and all his works. Then (having got that out of the way) he gets to business. One has the impression that if anyone in Dublin gets up and does something, the other intellectuals stand round and make destructive comments. And yet (so contradictory is human nature) this love of depreciation exists coincidentally with a display of mutual admiration which is positively disarming in its naïveté. Perhaps Congreve (who after all was educated at Trinity) was thinking more of Dublin than of London when he made one of his characters talk about "poets selling praise for praise and critics picking their pockets."

One of the most delightful aspects of Dublin life is its frugality and lack of ostentation. There is no "money standard" in Dublin, for no one, luckily, appears to have any money. An income of £600 or £700 a year, on which in London a single man with a moderate liking for the play, for dancing, and for entertaining his friends at restaurants would before the war have found it difficult to manage, in Dublin would be considered affluence. For one thing, the play, such as it is, is accessible for a few shillings; and the restaurant habit does not appear to have been developed at all. Dubliners are thrown entirely on their own wits to make their social life diverting, but it is safe to assert that Dublin hospitality (which is traditional) loses nothing from the fact that it lacks the oppressive opulence of London entertainment. Speaking from my own limited experience, I must say that I have never passed more amusing or delightful evenings than in the houses of friends in Dublin.

One of the reasons for the moderate standard of living in Dublin may be found in the fact that—execpt for the brewing of porter and the manufacture of whiskey and of biscuits—the city appears to have no industries. So far as I have been able to observe, the population of Dublin (not counting the brewers, &c.) is made up chiefly of doctors and priests, with a sprinkling of *rentiers*, a great horde of officials, and, finally, perhaps the largest proportion of abjectly poor people which is to be found in any city in Europe of the same size. The principal source of livelihood, alike for rich and poor, is undoubtedly that fine old crusted institution, the " Money

THE INTELLECTUALS 181

Office." The particular form of "Money Office" which supplies the necessities of the very poor has three golden balls hanging decoratively on its façade. Inside the establishment there is a long counter marked off by little partitions. Behind the counter wait the assistants who receive the quaint bundles presented to them—a patched woollen shawl, perhaps, enveloping a man's shirt, boots and Sunday trousers—and deliver in exchange to their owners the few shillings or pence necessary to support life or to procure forgetfulness. Among the very poor it is always the women who visit the pawnbroker, and every "Money Office" has its long list of regular clients.

The "Money Offices" for the intellectual and upper classes are naturally of far superior design, and no tell-tale golden balls detract from the dignity of their exteriors. They are maintained by the Government. They are housed in magnificent quarters. Merrion Street, Ely Place, Stephen's Green all contain these admirable institutions in which, for a certain number of hours each day, the intellectuals deposit their bodies, receiving for this act, from a grateful State, incomes ranging from about £200 to £4,000 per annum. Could one possibly conceive a more excellent, a more sensible, arrangement? I wish we had something of the kind in England, some such happy combination of ease with dignity for the deserving. In Dublin the road, for the educated young man, winds up hill all the way; and there are jobs for all who come. What in Heaven's name the Irish cultured classes would do if it were not for the lavish inefficiency of English administration I cannot imagine. Perhaps they would be forced to live by threatening to expose each other's washing!

The nervous strain occasioned by depositing oneself in these more elegant and Governmental "Money Offices" does not seem so excessive as to preclude the diversions of scholarship. In no other town have I encountered so many learned persons as I have in Dublin, or perhaps I should say, so many people able and willing to give "mixed company" the benefit of their erudition. The literary people, in particular, are sometimes tremendously impressive and awe-inspiring; so much so that it is occasionally rather a shock to trace them back not to a shelf of profound and epoch-making treatises but only to a few newspaper paragraphs or a single slender sheaf of verses. I cannot imagine a don at an English University, however distinguished he might be, inflicting his particular subject upon a collection of people composed largely of women and of obvious ignoramuses like myself. But in Dublin I have heard a "nut

THE INTELLECTUALS

of knowledge" keep an entire room in silence while he spouted ancient and modern Greek, and discussed the origins of Sanskrit, disgruntling a rival "nut" who knew something of these subjects, but couldn't get a word in edgeways, while the rest of us displayed on our faces that expression of "rapt attention" which we hope the other person will mistake for intelligent interest. Dropping Sanskrit for the moment, the Philologist went on to the derivation of names, relentlessly "deriving" all our names for us. One man had a name which was "patently Norse"; the name of a second was derived from the "low German"; and that of a third was a "French corruption."

"Now I have a nephew with rather a curious name," said a quiet woman with white hair, who had not previously spoken. "He was christened Judmar . . ."

"Judmar!" screamed the Philologist, "Judmar! Why that's obviously from the Kalmuck Jud*marah*, meaning 'shining warrior.' It occurs also in Tchali. I remember coming across the name Jud*maroosh* when I was living in Kajmackalan, among the Tchalis. Clearly the same name; but you note the subtle difference?"

We all sat round noting, as intelligently as we knew how, the "subtle difference."

When silence returned, the elderly lady

continued in the same even tones: " He was called Judmar because his mother had two favourite aunts, Judy and Mary. . . ." I was unable to hear how the Philologist extricated himself, but I feel sure that he did so with the greatest *aplomb*.

The collection of " knowledge," or intellectual *bricabracologie*, is no doubt as valuable a hobby as any other, but to make a custom of displaying the treasures of the collection at all times and in all seasons seems to me to have about it a certain flavour of provincialism. Another indication of provincial pedantry is to be found in the pronunciation of that, alas, household word, " margarine." In Dublin, even the people who sell it to you by the half-pound, pronounce the g hard, with one eye firmly fixed on the word's Greek derivation. It is almost as if they were speaking English like a dead language which they had acquired at Extension Lectures. In England, however, English is still far too much alive to permit of such a barbarity as pronouncing " margarine " with a hard g (thus turning it into an ugly word) when by pronouncing it with a soft g it makes quite a tolerable addition to the language. All the professors of all the universities may denounce this practice till they are blue in the face, but it will not make a penn'orth of difference; the community as a whole will continue to trust its ear, and to disregard everything else. If the word is to be assimilated into the English language it will be pronounced in the way which to the majority of English-speaking people seems most agreeable, and that sooner or later, inevitably becomes the *right* way.

The most widely dispersed form of learning (I will not say of pedantry) among the Dublin intellectuals seems to be a knowledge of Gaelic. The study of this language for Dubliners appears to have about it something quasi-religious—more than mere patriotism. As a means of having larks with the Government—some enthusiasts address all their letters in Gaelic, thus imposing the getting of wisdom on the Post Office—and as a means of emphasising nationalism by introducing a Gaelic equivalent which no one can read on to street name-boards, which are in any case usually illegible, one can understand it well enough. But no words of mine can express the solemnity displayed by some young Irishmen, particularly those who have been educated in England, in approaching this language which is not only not their mother tongue, but was not even the tongue of their grandmothers. I gather that (not counting the experts who burst into Gaelic at evening parties) nearly every Dublin intellectual has at one time or another coquetted with O'Growney's "First Steps." I myself, in a mood of commendable earnestness, got so far as to enquire where O'Growney's manuals could be purchased, and I hear that one of my fellow-countrymen, in the rapture of his conversion, has actually abjured all other languages save Irish. He is to be met with in the streets of Dublin in native Irish costume, brown kilt and sporran and all, and complete with blackthorn stick!

Before I had been in Dublin a month, when the glamour was still fresh, I prevailed on a youthful enthusiast who came to see me to read me some Gaelic love poems. I listened, all eagerness, anxiously waiting to be spellbound: but, alas, on that pellucid August evening the spell was not working. Now I have listened by the hour together to the *patois* they talk in the side streets of Amiens; to the peasants of the Cevennes who have no French; to Catalonian market women in Barcelona and in the narrow streets of Perignan; to Jugoslaves at Zara, at Ragusa, at Sebenico; to gabbling Montenegrin board-school boys on that white highway which leads down from Cettinje to Riecka. I have listened, entranced, while the poets of Les Baux said or sang their poems in the soft Provençal; and I have often heard about the extraordinary beauty of the Gaelic tongue, as it is spoken in the Western Highlands of Scotland. Yet I can safely say that never before in my life have I listened to anything so ear-torturing as the raucous sounds which emerged from my enthusiasts's gullet, as he relentlessly read on. I thought the poem would never end. A Gaelic love poem! I weep tears when I think of that lost, beautiful enthusiasm (acquired in London) which I unpacked from my suit-case after my arrival at North Wall. Alas! it died untimely: the Gaelic love poem slew it. The young man had in me no sceptic, but one all a-quiver to be enthralled by the sweet sounds with which I fondly expected to be charmed. I looked forward to being made emotional by seductive, crooning, unintelligible words as one is made emotional by hearing Italian or Spanish. But at all costs the truth must be confessed. Long before the love poem coughed, whined and spat itself to its conclusion I had fallen to thinking—of all languages in the world—of English. In those moments, with a kind of rapture, I rediscovered my native tongue. It seemed incredible that, political motives apart, the Irish could really wish to surrender the language of the Authorised Version, of Goldsmith and of Swift, of Mr. Yeats, even of Synge, a language which holds, collected and contained in it, all the various music of the centuries, for one which, whatever may be its beauties, remains archaic and uncouth. The music of English speech as compared with the Irish of the love poem suggested to my untutored mind the difference between, say, the Queen's Hall Orchestra and a Jew's harp. I mean no disrespect to the Jew's harp, which undoubtedly gives forth a certain eerie music of its own, lamentable and ghost-like. But though it may be loud or soft, it has essentially but one note. On the other hand, what infinite possibilities are there not in English? Of what millions of hungry human souls does it not satisfy the needs? It is the medium by which the thoughts of fully half the civilised world are conveyed and interchanged. And is there any language which can at moments be more musical, more languorous, more plaintive; at others fiercer, harder, more staccato? Think how our English words can be made to crackle down the page, banging and spitting hatred like Maxim guns; and again how they can be laid softly one after another, drooping with such a hunger of the soul as surely was never to be expressed in any other tongue. I own I cannot understand how an æsthetically sensitive people can carry its natural hatred of the sister island so far as to slight that most strangely complex and beautiful of living languages which happens to bear her name. English surely belongs no more exclusively to England than does French to France: both are priceless possessions of the human race, and to know either is to possess a key to a vast storehouse of treasure. In order to begin to appreciate English it is necessary to know a little French and to have at least a smattering of the classics. But it is not necessary to learn Irish. And since the study of English, like all studies which are worth beginning, can have no end—the man who says that he " knows English thoroughly " is a fool—I must confess that I cannot see much object in people for whom English happens to be the mother-tongue going side-tracking away trying to get the hang of Gaelic. It must be exceedingly difficult, for even my enthusiast was not, I believe, extremely proficient. However, when (after the reading of the love poem) I began stutteringly to mention some of the impressions which I have just stated, he pulverised me with a whole avalanche of facts out of his grammar book. Irish, he said, contained 187 more inflexions than any other European language, 57,000 more words, and so on. I bore up against the waves like a wall of concrete. To my own acute disappointment, I am even now unconvinced.

But if I am unable to grow enthusiastic about Gaelic, I have at least been profoundly impressed by those of the "Irish" Irish whom I have encountered in Dublin. The most noticeable thing about them is that they are good people, moved by noble impulses, austere and simple in their lives like men and women who have seen a vision and are filled with a deep purpose. Mistaken they may be in their political ideals (though I confess I do not believe it), but their sincerity shines out like a bright star in a dark night of corruption. It was from people of this kind that the leaders of the recent rebellion were drawn and from whom any further human sacrifices which the gods may demand of Ireland will doubtless be taken. It is not a pleasant thought for an Englishman; but then there is scarcely a page of Irish history which can provide pleasant thoughts for an Englishman. Perhaps that is why, with the strong commonsense which is said to distinguish his race, no Englishman ever reads one.

As for the " moderate " man in Irish politics, I confess he seems to me to be much the same as the moderate man everywhere else. The moderate man is always prone to compromise, to engage in political buying and selling. In Ireland he seems to be particularly adept at selling: perhaps that is the reason why he invariably prospers.

Throughout my stay in Dublin I have been unable to resist the conviction that it is the " Irish " Irish who hate us (or at least our Government) most bitterly whom we English ought most truly to respect. The clean fire of their loathing for oppression is just the fire which so much needs re-kindling in our own hearts. If we could but join them in the real " Holy War " not only would freedom come to Ireland, but to England herself might be restored all those qualities which in the past have made her great.

CHAPTER X.

Literature in Dublin.

I.

At a certain "literary evening," in reply to a question by Mr. George Russell about this book, I remarked, in an unguarded moment, that I proposed to spend the following morning at the National Library "with all the Irish poets on a table in front of me." Mr. Russell annihilated my timid conversational effort by observing (not without a trace of acidity in his tone) that if I proposed to do that it would have to be an exceedingly large table. I subsided, abashed, though indeed I had not intended to make any slighting reference to Ireland's poetic output. On the contrary, I had heard a great deal about modern Anglo-Irish verse in London and expected great things. Mr. Russell's remark made me feel I had badly put my foot in it by not expecting enough; so I resolved when I did get to the library that my researches should be more than perfunctory. Now I do not claim for a moment that I have looked into the works of every Irish writer who ever published verses, but as the result of Mr. Russell's retort I can say at least that I have explored some dozens of books which I should not otherwise have opened. Having emerged (a little exhausted) from this ordeal I must confess, with all respect, that if A. E. really considers that every fluent poetaster who writes rhymed rubbish and is vain enough to get it printed becomes a poet merely through the accident of Irish birth, I am unable to agree with him. The more hours I devote to reading Anglo-Irish poetry the more firmly convinced do I become that it would be possible to spend a morning at the National Library with the works (or rather the poetry) of all the Irish poets resting on my two knees.

I do not say this in any way to disparage Anglo-Irish poetry, for I am of those who consider an Irishman, Mr. W. B. Yeats, the greatest of living poets who write in English. When I take down a book of poems from my shelf to read for pleasure it is more likely than not to be a book by Mr. Yeats. And of the poets of lesser eminence who are more nearly my contemporaries I get certainly as much genuine delight from Mr. James Stephens' work as from that of any other modern writer. I suppose I have as good a claim to the " discovery " of Mr. James Stephens as anyone else in England, for when a review copy of "Insurrections" reached me, I think in 1909, some days before publication, I at once wrote a notice of it as enthusiastic and as lengthy as my editor would allow. Moreover, when the individual who in those days used to visit my flat with a black bag and carry away my review copies tried to carry off that slender brown volume with the others it was promptly, almost fiercely, rescued. I can imagine no more touching tribute! Before I came to Dublin my acquaintance with modern Anglo-Irish poetry was limited to the works of Mr. Yeats, of Synge and of Mr. Stephens, all of whom I cherished; to the outside cover of A. E.'s poems, which I had been repeatedly advised to admire; to Lord Dunsany's fantasies which I had read in the "Saturday Review"; to Miss Moira O'Neill's "Songs of the Glens of Antrim"; and to some of the poetry of Thomas McDonagh which I read at the time of the rebellion. I had, therefore, a great many new poetic acquaintances to make. Since in literary circles in London everything Irish was tremendously in vogue when I left, it was in a mood of thrilled expectancy that I sat myself at a table in the dim penetralia of the National Library with about fifty slender volumes in front of me—a first instalment. Before I began on any of them I sat ruminating for a while, trying to collect my ideas about

Ireland's total contribution to literature in English, with a view to discovering to what precisely it amounted. I had heard so much of the literary genius of the Irish race (both in London and also in Dublin), of " Ireland's Literary Renaissance " and so forth, that I had accepted, without testing it in any way, the theory of Irish supremacy at least in the art of poetry.

I cannot claim to be a " deep " reader; but I daresay I have read as widely as most people who care for letters and who live by writing. So I sat and cudgelled my brains for those great Irish names of the past three centuries by whom the foundations of the prestige of Anglo-Irish literature must of course have been laid. It was ages before I could think of anyone at all except Mr. Yeats, J. M. Synge, Mr. George Moore and Bernard Shaw—all moderns. At last I remembered that Goldsmith, for all his English-sounding name, had been born in Ireland. I grudged the Irish that dear soul, but in any case there was one great name for them. Then there were Swift and Burke and Sheridan and the illustrious Berkeley in the same century; and in the century before I remembered that Congreve and Farquhar had something Irish about them. But where had all these great Irish poets disappeared to? I recalled one or two moving poems by James Clarence Mangan,

Tom Moore's amiable ditties, and a great mass of patriotic or nationalist verse the value of which was sentimental and historical rather than literary—Davis, Gerald Griffin and people of that sort. Then in the last century there were a number of names chiefly of local importance and of no special interest for the general reader—Ferguson, Callanan, O'Shaughnessy, and such like. But where on earth were the *great* poets, great in the sense that Keats, Byron, Coleridge, Shelley are great? There must be some great Irish poets, I said to myself, for to think of Ireland nowadays is to think of poetry. Cursing my feeble memory I consulted Sir Arthur Quiller-Couch's execrable anthology, which is at least inclusive in regard to names. Nobody of real eminence up to 1860 could have escaped him. To my consternation I discovered that out of all that great company in "The Oxford Book of English Verse" there were scarcely more than twenty Irish names. And of those twenty only Goldsmith and Yeats seemed to me of real importance.

Having failed with poetry, I turned to novels. Surely Ireland, which at least before the Famine had a larger population than Scotland, must have produced as many novelists. There were Lever and Lover of course—but the first and better of these two was practically an Englishman, the son of an English architect and builder who worked on the construction of the Custom House under Gandon. Then there was Goldsmith again, and Maria Edgworth, and later on William Carleton whose works I have never attempted but whose face in the National Portrait Gallery inspires confidence. After that I could only think of Sheridan Lefanu, of Mrs. B. M. Croker (humph!), the Misses Somerville and Ross, Emily Lawless, Jane Barlow Canon Hannay, Katharine Tynan and—incomparably the greatest of them all—George Moore. So just as in poetry there was no one of importance between Goldsmith and Yeats, so in prose fiction there was no name of importance between Goldsmith and George Moore! Where on earth had all these Irish geniuses hidden themselves? My cogitations (assisted by formidable works of reference) resulted in the rather staggering conclusion that from the literary point of view Ireland had a deal of lee-way to make up, and that her much trumpeted " literary Renaissance " was at least a century overdue. The Irish had always, however, been admired for their wit, for their mastery of the spoken word, their remarkable gift of talk; and that perhaps accounted for the fact that the one branch of literary art of which they had produced a number of first-rate exponents was the art of writing comedy. Here we had a series of great names—Congreve, Goldsmith, Sheridan, Oscar Wilde, Bernard Shaw! But as for Ireland's poetical reputation, well everything depended on this famous " Renaissance."

I looked again at the volumes on the table in front of me. On whom should I begin? Finding that so many of them had been ushered into the world under the protecting wing of Mr. Russell, it occurred to me that I could not do better than start off on A. E. himself.

II.

" THE first thing to do, when setting out to criticise a book "—thus I was instructed in my youth by a famous critic—" is to forget everything you may know about the personality of its author. A book is a separate thing, with an existence of its own entirely distinct from that of the man who made it. It must be judged, therefore, strictly on its own merits, without reference to its author's virtues or defects. How absurd, for example, it would be to condemn Oscar Wilde's plays because of his morals! How ridiculous to laud the poems of Miss Ella Wheeler Wilcox because of her sincere piety; or to imitate the literary style of Viscount Footle merely because he has a seat in the House of Lords! The word ' publication' implies that a volume has been sent out into the open sea of public criticism, to take its chance, just as the words 'for private circulation only' imply that no such risks are contemplated. If a critic is to be honest he must be perfectly detached (in other words, no respecter of persons), and no criticism is worthy of the name which is not honest and unbiassed. You may take it from me that an author who resents honest criticism of his work, however severe the criticism may be, is usually an impostor and invariably a fool. Without criticism—which is an art founded on the other arts and worthy to rank with any of them—writers would languish in the sickly fumes of mutual admiration; and literature would die. To sum up, the task of the critic is to test the work submitted to him in accordance with whatever standard of values he possesses, and then to make a detailed and strictly accurate statement of the result of that test. . . ."

I record these impressive platitudes at length and as nearly as possible in the speaker's own words because, commonplace as they may seem, it is astonishing how difficult his directions are to put into practice, how fraught with danger is the very attempt to do so. See how few of us who venture on the thankless task, succeed! Reviewing my own past reviewers for a moment, I must (to be truthful) confess that some of those who have treated me most severely have seemed the most deserving of respect. I think the hardest knocks I ever received were delivered once by a writer in *The Nation*—an admirable piece of destructive criticism, impersonal, witty, and too terribly full of perception to be at all comfortable. A familiar and quite different type of reviewer is the merely ill-mannered, the man whose face you would like to walk on. I have a cherished *bête noire* belonging to this variety—a gentleman of High Church proclivities, one of whose poems some years ago I rejected for publication in a monthly paper. Since that unlucky day he has lain in wait for my books like a hungry crocodile. When they appear he claims them from all the newspapers he can and uses up his space not in slating them—a perfectly legitimate proceeding—but in calling their author odious names. His is an example of the " personal " or libellous method: he does it to annoy. Another type of reviewer, almost equally familiar to most of us, is the well-meaning friend who never fails to find one's feeblest work " masterly in construction " and " brilliantly carried out." Him I distrust tenderly. To read him is like eating a pound and a half of mixed chocolates at a sitting. You don't feel quite sure of how you do feel: your digestion gives you curious qualms. And then, last of all, there is the unknown appreciative critic for whom we all sigh and whom few of us are lucky enough to encounter as often as we should like. On the whole, I think the reviewers who make an attempt to observe the rules of the game are in an honourable minority. It would be instructive to see what would happen to a work of genius by a "Hun" if one were to be published in English to-day; or what the newspapers would make of Shakespeare if his works were just out and he were known to be "pacifist"!

So far as I have been able to make a comparison between London and Dublin in the matter of criticism, it seems to me that Londoners incline to be much more drastic and outspoken on paper about Londoners than the Dublin critics are about their fellow-townsmen. The Dubliner will strafe the foreign foe readily enough; but about the work of his own literary acquaintances he tends to have two sets of opinions, one for public display, the other for private interchange. The reason for this probably is that Dublin is a small town where every writer knows every critic, London a vast urban nation where authors and their judges are usually strangers to one another. It is obviously much easier to be "detached" about someone whom you have never seen, and much—very much—easier to be honest and unbiassed in writing of a man whom you expect never to meet.

I discovered the truth of this, to my cost, when I sat down to explore modern Irish verse in the National Library. Many of the volumes at once recalled the face and form of some agreeable acquaintance; and in writing of A. E., that kindly, dominating figure, how should one hope to achieve complete detachment? The attempt must be made, however, for the sole *raison d'être* of this volume is that it should form a truthful and honest record of impressions. Resolutely banishing from my mind, therefore, all thought of Mr. Russell I took up " The Collected Poems of A. E.," and read them through.

The volume is not an easy one to read from cover to cover at a sitting, and perhaps I ought not to have made the attempt, for A. E. is a poet whose verse it is easier to appreciate in small doses. The titles of his poems given in the list of contents are calculated to terrify most readers in anticipation. Here are a few of them : Truth, Duality, Dusk, Night, Dawn, Day, Desire, Rest, Pity, Dream, Love, Immortality, Symbolism, Sacrifice, Brotherhood, The Earth, Prayer, Benediction, The Morning Star, Destiny, Tragedy, Unity, Content, Reconciliation. What gigantic themes; what sublime courage the poet must possess thus to assail them by frontal attack! I turned eagerly to these poems and read them, together with a great many more with similar titles, only to find my disappointment increasing. No: I could not come under their spell, try how I would. With the esoteric religious thought underlying many of them I was more or less familiar, for about fifteen years ago I read Mr. A. P. Sinnett's book "Esoteric Buddhism," and the ideas absorbed at that time have remained with me ever since. But it did not seem to me that Mr. Russell's poems clothed his thoughts with the inevitable words, in such a way as to transmute them into great poetry. The themes were transcendental enough but the language often undistinguished and the verification dangerously facile. I would not for one moment be so presumptuous as to question the inspiration of one who seems so completely at his ease before the Great White Throne as A. E.; but it does seem to me that it is often by the significance which a poet can give to simple things, to apparently trivial (but actual) things that he is able to be most revealing. The method has also an alluring shyness about it, a kind of diffidence which develops in the reader, without any self-consciousness on his part, all of which he is capable in the way of spiritual understanding. A. E. seems to set out to transcribe directly into words the soul-state which music or great poetry sometimes induces; but he has no magic to induce it himself. His method is direct, not oblique. He states, however vaguely, rather than suggests. And as all his statements are definitely "mystic" in character (or else, one feels, he would never trouble to make them in verse) the effect of them is apt to be overpowering rather than helpful. A friend said to me recently that A. E.'s poetry reminded her of eating honey out of a pot with a spoon; which is perhaps a better way of making the same point. . . .

Never was there a book of verses more full of "sleep," "peace," "dreams," "stars," "twilit trees," "God's Planets," "Clouds," "Quietness," "Holies of Holies," than A. E.'s "Collected Poems." But you don't convey these things to the mind merely by mentioning them. And sometimes the essential truths on which A. E. likes to dwell are more comfortably to be read in sacred books, where their clothing of language is apt to have a certain homespun simplicity or sober quaintness. I say more comfortably, having in mind lines like the following :

"Your eyes, your other eyes of dream
Looked at me through the veil of blank."

There is nothing in the thought that inspires one to laughter or makes a grin excusable. Yet it is distinctly uncomfortable to bump against a phrase like "veil of blank."

The effect of a whole volume constantly on the most exalted note is inevitably monotonous. The effect on me of A. E.'s poems is almost exactly similar to that of the paintings of the most advanced school of post-impressionist painters. Mr. Russell's poems (except superficially; he has not discarded ordinary verse-forms) with their elimination of the actual and their evident intention of giving the very essence of the essential, might have been built up in accordance with half the recent manifestoes. If Kandinsky were a poet he would belong roughly to the same school as Mr. Russell. The post-impressionists—Vorticists, Cubists, Futurists and such-like—all aim at representing the mulishness of the mule, the horseyness of the horse, the significance of the anecdote rather than the anecdote itself. In painting a portrait of Mr. Smith, they will try to indicate the spiritual effect on them of Mr. Smith's "Smithishness," so that you will look in vain for any attempt to reproduce his outward features. Mr. Russell's poetry has obvious affinities with all this. In both cases the intention is beyond praise; but the results are apt to be disappointing.

As I think over the great poets whose work I have read (and Mr. Russell's verse at least claims comparison only with that of the great, even if it be to his disadvantage as an artist) it seems to me that the most " sublime " of them have always approached warily the Holy of Holies. The reader's thoughts are led on stage by stage, with the help of beautiful imagery or by clearly outlined pictures, until at last, with a greatness of effect which is the measure of the greatness of the poetry, of the genius with which the contrasting shadows have been massed, he comes face to face with the illumination of the inspired climax. Suddenly, when perhaps his reader is expecting it least, the great poet flings wide the magic casements. In A. E.'s poetry, however, there is never any climax, never any contrast, and the light is all the while so dazzling that very often we can see nothing at all. The expression in verse of religious ideas, however profound or even poetic those ideas may be, is not quite the same thing as writing poetry. And just as a good poem has been written about a flea on a lady's bonnet, so also much verse which is not poetry at all has been made upon the Cosmos, upon the swirling of the planets, upon the moon and stars. At his best, as in poems like " Reconciliation " with its fine opening line:

" I begin once again through the grass to be bound to the Lord——"

A. E.'s poetry seems to me to achieve a music sonorous, organ-like in its quality. My disappointment was due, I think, to the fact that I compared his work unconsciously with all the very greatest poetry which I had ever read in English. After spending a few hours among some of his disciples, however, I must admit that I felt inclined to return and blot out what I had written and hail him as a master. For at least A. E.'s poetry (whether you like it or whether you don't) is unique of its kind, and it does express his own personality and no one else's.

After investigating Mr. Russell's verses I began next on Mr. Darrell Figgis. I opened his book, "The Mount of Transfiguration" with loud anticipatory groans. I remembered an earlier volume of his—the name of it has escaped me, but it had a preface by Mr. G. K. Chesterton and it was heavier than lead. The new book seemed at first quite to live up to my forebodings. I opened on some dedicatory verses addressed in homage to A. E., in which the poet claimed to have seen

" . . . the shining powers that lurk and sway
  Behind the changing show their gestures raise."

How one distrusts the spiritual insight of these people who are so ready to bleat about their mystic visions! One distrusts them just as one distrusts the piety of the spinster who attends all the services at the parish church and lets you know it; just as one does *not* distrust the wisdom of the simple and unpretentious—nurses, shepherds and gay old people. Has Mr. Figgis seen all this (as he asserts with such confidence) or has he merely read A. E. and felt that he ought to have seen it? His book opens with a poem called "The Rencounter," and soon after this oppressive gallicism we come upon the phrase "in colours tristful" (ugh!) which has of course to rhyme with "wistful" lower down. But Mr. Figgis gets better in his "Songs of Acaill." Here he sometimes takes the trouble to use his eyes and now and then has the virility to be exact when it would be less bother to be vague. "Curlew and wild geese cried in the upper air," he writes, instead of "the wild birds cried," or something equally empty. Curlew and wild geese are things beautiful to think about, and the phrase "in the upper air" helps one to visualize them. Here for a moment he escapes his lazy and exasperating Celtic vagueness. This "vagueness," this feeling of having "nothing to catch hold of" is—after all—not to be noted in any great poetry or indeed in any poetry at all that is worthy of the name. I opened one of Mr. Yeats' books absolutely at random:

" The old brown thorn trees break in two high
　　over Cummen Strand,
　　Under a bitter black wind that blows from
　　the left hand. . . ."

Isn't the imagination gripped by it at once? The reader's attention is immediately arrested, the brain is set working and the spell which true poetry always exercises begins to take hold of him. Here in a couple of lines we have something which it would be impossible to paraphrase adequately in twenty—a complete and vivid picture, full of suggestion. And all the time we are really just as near those " shining powers that lurk and sway behind the changing show their gestures raise," which Mr. Figgis wrote about, as we could have been by any method of direct approach We can do the direct approach for ourselves once the poet has shown us the way, as it is his function to do.

After the " Songs of Acaill " I began Mr. Figgis' book again at the end and discovered two terrible efforts. One was called " Day," the other " Night." Here is a stanza from " Night ":

"Wrapt in the mantle of the Night
 At the hosting of the stars,
I would forget Time's trivial flight
Or that the soul hath bars,
And furled with wide infinity
Gather all wisdom unto me."

Alas, what dreary cliché stuff it is! Is there any educated man with the habit of writing who could not turn it out by the cabfull if he gave his mind to it? It seems as if A. E. will have much to answer for on the Day of Judgment; perhaps he occasionally mur-

murs to himself "save me from my disciples!" I think there must be a school of critics in Ireland (and perhaps in England as well) from whom some of the poets take their cue, who cling to the belief that all that is necessary in order to create a "Celtic" poem is to stuff some verses full of words like "night," "dawn," "glimmering," "twilight," "shadowy," "gray." Bundle all this claptrap together anyhow, cut it into lengths and make it rhyme: and there you are! Leaving "Day" and "Night" I came upon a "Ballad of Dead Lovers:"

> "Oh love of loves! Oh lips so pure!
> Oh, eyes so full of joy at me!
> Oh, breasts so exquisite in their lure!
> Oh, flesh so white in its sanctity!"

After this I read some bad "Bacchanals," and a long and dreary poem whose name I forget, and arriving again at the "Songs of Acaill" felt that Mr. Figgis might be a poet after all, somehow somewhen.

From Mr. Figgis I turned to Seumas O'Sullivan's "Poems," and was soon captivated by their fragile, sometimes rather anæmic decadence. He struck me as being a kind of Celtic Dowson, but with a colder and thinner music at his command. There was the same gloating over pretty words, however, and much the same religious feeling—that is to say a sensuons appreciation of the outward forms of Catholicism. Such a line as " A wisdom winnowed from light words " would surely have pleased Dowson, who might have written it himself. The following little poem gives a good idea of the poet's strength and weakness:

"I go with silent feet and slow
  As all my black-robed brothers go;
  I dig awhile and read and pray,
  So portion out my pious day
  Until the evening time and then
  Work at my book with cunning pen.
  If she should turn to me awhile,
  If she would turn to me and smile,
  My book would be no more to me
  Than some forgotten phantasy,
  And God no more unto my mind
  Than a dead leaf upon the wind."

This, although it is called " The Monk," really gives a photographically accurate picture of the decadent of the eighteen-nineties who was not only quite prepared to give up God for any fatuous or trivial reason, but was always boasting about it. It must be confessed that, in spite of their superficial attractiveness, their verbal felicities and technical dexterity, there is a certain ingrained feebleness of thought in most of Seumas O'Sullivan's poems which robs them of complete success. And his books lack colour; they are grey, etiolated. He seems to have suffered badly from the cotton-wool mists of the Celtic twilight. He is rarely exact in his observation of detail. I see that Mr. Ernest Boyd in his very interesting book on "Ireland's Literary Renaissance" has accused Mr. O'Sullivan of being "saturated with wistfulness;" and it must be admitted that the charge is justified. "Twilight flocks," "faint forms of the beloved dead" and so on leave a kind of snail-track of wistfulness across his pages. But his decadent fastidiousness comes to his aid even here, and saves him where some of his contemporaries (with less of the artist in them) are lost. Here is an example of a stanza which he has just managed to rescue from the bogs of wistfulness:

"Twilight people why will you still be crying
Crying and calling to me out of the trees?
For under the quiet grass the wise are lying,
And all the strong ones are gone over the
　　seas."

And here a whole poem, similarly rescued, called "The Starling Lake":

"My sorrow that I am not by the little dun
By the lake of the starlings at Rosses under
　　the hill,
And the larks there, singing over the fields of
　　dew,
Or evening there and the sedges still.

For plain I see now the length of the yellow sand,
And Lissadell far off and its leafy ways,
And the holy mountain whose mighty heart
Gathers into it all the coloured days.

My sorrow that I am not by the little dun,
By the lake of the starlings at evening when all is still,
And still in whispering sedges the herons stand.
'Tis there I would nestle at rest till the quivering moon
Uprose in the golden quiet over the hill."

"The Fiddler" and "The Piper" are pleasant lyrics, and in the piece called "St. Anthony" Mr. O'Sullivan seems to have had a fine inspiration, but to have waited till that inspiration cooled before beginning to write down his poem.

Mr. O'Sullivan has two manners: one "shadowy" and "twilit," the other realistic. There can be no doubt that the first of these is the manner which suits him best. He is not a good realist. He seems to have attempted realism as a kind of penance, as an effort to check his tendency to flop into wistfulness. I have a particular grudge against one of his realistic poems which describes the singing of a lark in a slum street because of a reference in it to the "organ's blasphemy of sound."

If a poet is going to write about the mean streets he ought to study their natural history, their flora and fauna. Now the barrel-organ is a thing rich in colour (just what Mr. O'Sullivan's poetry lacks), and in most big cities it plays an important part in the life of the slums. To the poor it means a great deal, at least to the London poor, who gladly give their ha'pence to the smiling hurdy-gurdy man who flashes his white teeth at them while they dance. Personally I have scant sympathy with the superior people who tear their hair at the sound of the street-organ. Many pretty feet, even in the most select neighbourhoods, have been set dancing (in private of course) by its cheery, metallic tunes. The hurdy-gurdy is most welcome, perhaps, when he arrives at bath-time. Blessings on his "blasphemy of sound" which makes staid persons skip like rams and do toe-dancing across the bathroom floor. Surely Mr. O'Sullivan can appreciate the lark without having at the same time to abuse the poor organ-grinder? I was much relieved to see that he made amends in "Nelson Street" and "From an Epistle."

From Seumas O'Sullivan I strayed to Mr. Campbell's "Irishry," attracted by his preface which seemed to promise a refuge from shadowy glimmers. "Artists," he writes, "are fortunate in that the colour of Irish life is still radiant. One hears on all sides of greyness, emigration, degeneracy, but one has only to look about to see that the cry has no mouth. There is blood everywhere; in the boglands of Connacht, as well as on the farms of Leinster; in the streets of Cork as well as in that barbarous nook Belfast, my own calf-ground." All this is like a breath of fresh air; but it does not prevent Mr. Campbell from writing thus about a shepherd:

> "   . . . the cloudy bars
> Of nebulae, the constellations ring
> His forehead like a king."

However, he soon drops this, and lives up to his preface, giving us vivid character sketches of Irish types—" The Unfrocked Priest," "The Tinkers," " The Exile," " The Fairies," " The Gombeen," "The Ploughman," etc.—which are full of colour and vitality.

After Mr. Campbell I attacked a whole host of little books of verse, which hardly differed in any way from our London output. Professor Dowden's graceful poems seemed to be rather like what the poems of a Professor would be like; Katharine Tynan's many little books were clearly of the " harmless " description— fluent, facile, pretty-pretty; Mr. T. W. Rolleston's scholarly " Sea-Spray " contained one good poem; and many other books of verse by other hands contained no poems at all. I found a beautiful religious note both in Miss Susan L. Mitchell's "The Living Chalice," and also in Miss Eva Gore-Booth's various volumes. These last two poets seemed to show a far deeper religious feeling than Katharine Tynan, and at the same time to be more distinctively in the "Irish mode." It was after leaving Miss Gore-Booth that I suddenly encountered Mr. Lysaght. Of all the figures to loom towards me out of the Celtic twilight his was assuredly the most unexpected. He greets his readers with a loud, robust "Hallo." His brow is wet with honest sweat; and I should imagine he was never wistful, even for a moment, in the whole of his life. He leans on his "four-pronged fork"; he writes of a heifer being delivered of a stubborn first-born calf; and of tending a suffering horse's colic. It is a little depressing to find him almost in the next breath filling up space with such clichés as "Life is not all fun and frolic," "harum-scarum throngs," and so on. At times, too, his naïveté is positively disarming:

"'Twas like the sudden glorious discovery
 A man makes when he finds he loves a
    woman."

His worst moments are when he becomes literary or "art simple," as in his references to "The King in his Parliament Shop," or "The Pope that's in Rome." He is at his best in vivid, homely pictures of farm life, minutely observed. Take the following, for example, from "The March Fair."

> "Herded with others, scores and scores
> Our bullocks mixed with cows and stores
> Are driven through the thronging fair
> Out to the railway station, where
> Numbers of trucks, all just the same,
> Swallow the beasts we knew by name."

And here is another picture precise and yet tender:—

> "And in the luscious pastures stand my kine,
> Some suckle calves, some plod home to the byre.
> Bullocks knee-deep in pasture graze their fill
> Or seek the shallows in a careless line,
> Or under shady branches lie quite still
> Chewing the cud with jaws that never tire."

Mr. Lysaght is admirable when he writes about his cows, his ass, his grey horse. But in his poem "To my Dog," in order to assure us and himself of the virtues of his own simplicity, he must needs start abusing other people : —

"Those who prate of their bags and their battues and drives,
Who ride to their moors and their coverts in motors
And chat while they wait to other men's wives. . . ."

Faugh, the filthy fellows! Fancy their having the lewdness to chat (while they waited) with *other men's wives*! That's what comes of keeping motors, of course. If they had been real gentlemen they would have shut their mugs, stared at the ladies in silent contempt and generally shown a decent respect for the rights of private property. But Mr. Lysaght is rarely as fatuous as this, and it is a shame to pounce on a moment of aberration in what is a delightful and very winning book. Its literary value, as the quotations have shown, is uneven; but the personality revealed all through is invariably attractive. One last word, *do* minnows "dream"—except when they have to rhyme with "stream"? When I was a small boy they seemed to dart about continuously, even in the hottest sunshine; but perhaps the Irish minnow is more languid.

From Mr. Lysaght I went to another rustic poet who has been greatly boomed in England, in Poetry Bookshop circles—Mr. Francis

Ledwidge. I began on his "Songs of the Fields," and read it all through, and afterwards couldn't remember anything at all about it. So I opened it again and found some tenuous little poems, some of them pretty enough—"A Song of April," for example, and "The Sister"—but strangely lacking (as it seemed to me) in any real savour of the fields. And the book had a great big introduction to it by Lord Dunsany—in fact, I have never picked up a volume which looked more like a book of poems. Afterwards I read "Songs of Peace" by the same hand, which also had an introduction by Lord Dunsany. The book opens with a long poem, "A Dream of Artemis," and is divided into sections headed "In Barracks," "In Camp," "At Sea," "In Serbia," "In Greece," "In Hospital," "In Egypt." These topical indications of where the poems were composed are interesting, for surely never were purer or more peaceful verses written amid the horrors of war. I did not find anything of much poetic value in either of Mr. Ledwidge's volumes; but occasionally he achieves a pretty phrase—"From its blue vase the rose of evening drops," for instance—and both his books breathe a spirit of gentleness and purity which reminds one at times of Mr. W. H. Davies.

It is in some ways a far cry from Mr.

Ledwidge to Miss Letts. Miss Letts is not an "art" poet, she is frequently sentimental, seldom attempts more than the merely pretty, and never twangs at too unmanageable a harp. She makes her servant girl talk about being "lost without the bogland and lost without the sea, and the harbour and the fishing-boats that sail out fine and free." Alas, one suspects that the little maid was really more likely to be thinking of the "Pictures," which are apt to be more thrilling to young persons from the country than those memories of boglands, etc., so dear to the cultivated urban mind. But this is hyper-criticism, no doubt. Miss Letts has a sense of character, also a sense of humour. Her verse flows easily and is readable, and is greatly helped by the use of evocative proper names.

The work of Patrick McGill, author of "Songs of the Dead End" and many other books of verse and prose, seems at first to have an attractive actuality; but his poetry, at all events, is really often far more sloppily sentimental than that of Miss Letts. Listen to this from "The Old Lure":

> "When I go back to the old pals
> 'Tis a glad, glad boy I'll be;
> With them will I share the doss-house bunk,
> And join their revels with glee;
> And the lean men of the loan shacks
> Shall share their tucker with me."

Don't you believe it! That bunkum is written to thrill young ladies in suburbs. Mr. McGill no more sighs for a doss-house bunk than any other sensible man who has enjoyed clean sheets. However, to gain a literary reputation in London a writer has only to remember and record minutely an unconventional experience. (Was not Mr. McGill extensively advertised as the " Navvy " poet?). Lines like the following are enough to make a certain school of London critics swoon in ecstacy :--

"Dibble and drift and drill,
Rachet and rail and rod,
Shovel and spanner and screw,
Hard-hafted hammer and hod."

And indeed this catalogue is more tolerable than mere "shadowy" slip-slop; though it isn't poetry either.

When I returned to my table after an interval of several days, I began on Dora Sigerson Shorter, who struck me as being an excellent craftsman with a faculty for writing good straightforward ballads, and enough self-criticism to prevent her from attempting more than she can reasonably hope to accomplish. And her work breathes a love for the country of her birth, which must endear it to her compatriots. But Miss Alice Milligan!—she is on fire with a national feeling which sweeps the reader off his feet. I did not know the name of this poet, and opened her little brown volume "Hero Lays" in a mood of apathy. The apathy gave way to excitement in a moment. Some of her poems are enough to make any Englishman—for the English are terribly prone to this kind of thing—long to be allowed to become a naturalised Sinn Feiner and to die fighting against the British tyrants until, with a shock, he realises that this would be siding with the little vulgar boys against Auntie (God bless her!). It is all very confusing.

"When I was a little Girl" is the sort of poem which no Englishman could, I think, read without a stirring of the blood. I wonder if the Irish will ever realise how dear is the thought of rebellion against oppression to the English spirit. If only they would do so, what a warm friendship might spring up between the two nations, and how successfully they might combine to exterminate oppressors!

> "But one little rebel there,
> Watching all with laughter,
> Thought "When the Fenians come
> I'll rise and go after."
>
> Wished she had been a boy,
> And a good deal older ——
> Able to walk for miles
> With a gun on her shoulder.

> Able to lift aloft
> That green flag o'er them
> (Red coats and black police
> Flying before them).
>
> And as she dropped asleep,
> Was wondering whether
> God, if they prayed to Him,
> Would give fine weather."

From Miss Milligan it was a depressing descent to Mr. James H. Cousins, by whom I read some smooth verse dealing with Irish legends—"Etain the Beloved" and so on—and some sonnets about Heaven and Earth and Love's Infinity, all rather empty and meaningless. Afterwards (still abashed by Mr. Russell's remark about the infinite number of the Irish poets) I trudged through many more volumes of minor verse. It all scanned and rhymed and displayed much study of metres; but the general effect of it was like some new chemical process for creating a vacuum. And then, just when I was beginning to wilt from sheer exhaustion, I opened one of the smallest of the books in front of me, in the middle, and came on these lines:

> "The city clocks point out the hours,
>   They look like moons on the darkest towers."

A human voice at last—it was Padraic Colum's—and I began at the beginning and read the book all through, finding it full of beautiful and curious things. "The Suilier" is a strange poem, and here is a verse from "The Drover":

> "Then the wet winding roads,
> Brown bogs with black water;
> And my thoughts on white ships,
> And the King o' Spain's daughter."

And here again are some lines from "An Old Woman of the Roads":—

> "O, to have a little house
> To own the hearth and stool and all
> The heaped up sods upon the fire
> The pile of turf again' the wall!
> To have a clock with weights and chains
> And pendulum swinging up and down!"

To come on Mr. Colum after so much dreary tramping along the characterless *routes nationales* of minor Celtic verse was like taking a sudden plunge across the moors and catching the will o' the wisp in the palm of your hand.

After my discovery of Padraic Colum I did not make many more researches among unfamiliar names. I re-read the verse of Thomas MacDonagh, finding again in it many beauties of thought and sometimes traces of that haunting music which he has himself described as the "Irish mode." "The Yellow Bittern" struck me as being a particularly lovely poem. Joseph Plunkett's verses seemed, however, less spontaneous, more scholarly and mannered, and far less interesting, save for the tragic interest which will always surround them. It was a great pleasure to re-read Moira O'Neill's curiously touching "Songs from the Glens of Antrim"; and to renew my acquaintance with Lord Dunsany's rather precious fantasies which reveal a distinct and distinguished personality. "And Fame turned her back on him and walked away; but in departing she looked over her shoulder and smiled at him as she had not smiled before, and, almost speaking in a whisper, said:

'I will meet you in the graveyard at the back of the workhouse, in a hundred years.'"

It was a great delight to get back once more to familiar ground, to Synge, to W. B. Yeats, to James Stephens. My long hours of research had yielded me but two poets whom I should regret to have missed, Alice Milligan and Padraic Colum; and it had given me an invincible distaste (I confess it with grief) for all "Celtic" verse which falls below the standard set by its greatest living exponents. I defy anyone who reads modern Irish poetry

P

in big doses not to have a surfeit of "twilight," of "greyness," "glimmerings," "dreams," "star-hostings," and what not. These "dreams" cannot all be authentic. One feels convinced that some of them are due more to an unwise diet than to the midnight wanderings of the soul. The finest antidote I can conceive for too much "twilight" is to spend an hour or two with Mr. Stephens' books.

In Mr. Stephens' poetry we are transported to the Infinite by contact with the Actual. No poet understands better than he the nearness to God of the child, nor what a little divil he can be at the same time. There is always an impish, freakish note in his poetry which cuts through the materialism of the mind like wire through cheese. And his poetry, without preliminary flourish of trumpets or display of spiritual "swank," seems to have the faculty of liberating the reader's thought. He is not a despiser of poor bad men; he has some of that instinctive sympathy with all human creatures which is perhaps the chief message which Russian literature has for Western Europe. "Superiority," the superiority which must épater le bourgeois, sneer at the "philistine" and howl imprecations at that class of the community from which almost every great artist who ever lived has sprung, is surely the besetting sin of all modern English literature. But Mr. Stephens is singularly free from it; he doesn't deal out half-bricks even at England with any enthusiasm. At least, unlike many Irish people, he does not confuse the English nation with a handful of English bureaucrats. And he sings thus in "The Adventures of Seumas Beg":

"When no flower is nigh you might
Spy a weed with deep delight;
So, when far from saints and bliss,
God might give a sin a kiss."

A stranger may well fancy that he finds in Mr. Stephens' poetry and in his prose stories a breath from the most ancient Ireland, pure and uncontaminated by any of those foreign influences which for so many centuries have tended to swamp and drown the true, the lovely Irish voice. No Irishman has perhaps done more than Dr. Douglas Hyde to preserve and recapture this true Irish voice. I have not referred before to Dr. Douglas Hyde's "Love Songs from Connacht" because, unlike the great mass of modern Irish verse which derives its inspiration from them, they seem outside the range of a stranger's criticism. I can only say that, more than any other book which I have read since I have been in Dublin, the "Love Songs from Connacht" helped me to appreciate the following passage in a letter which I received from a friend soon after I came to Ireland:

"And now you are in a country whose ancient civilisation still charms the contemplative mind. Like some age-worn jewel, scratched and dulled maybe by coarse, brutal, alien hands through which it has passed, it still charms the eye of the discerning who perceive in it a purity and brilliance, an interest and a magic infinitely more alluring and significant than all the dazzles shining on the chest and the poll of the rich brewer's wife. Yes: the fragrance which still lingers of that old Dawn in Ireland will indeed train and test your Saxon nose. That fragrance drew and charmed the sons of the Great William who crossed the sea to clump the stolid Saxon on the head—charmed them and drew them so that they became the brothers of those ancient ones, intimate, indistinguishable, mated in a true race-marriage. That fragrance still lingers in the land where the divine arts of song and dance were honoured and understood many, very many, centuries before the Renaissance—that period of menace and misfortune for Ireland. . . ."

III.

In the course of my self-conducted Cook's tour round Ireland's Literary Renaissance, I came upon an enormous quantity of verse; a large output of plays, political treatises and books about Ireland; but extremely few novels. The energy which English writers store up, by living lives of glum taciturnity and aloofness, to put into novel writing, Irish authors seem to send up the chimney like smoke in a steady stream of brilliant talk. I would sooner spend an evening with any tenth-rate Irish poet than with the greatest living English novelist. The English ideal is expressed in the story printed on a popular brand of tobacco, of the meeting between Carlyle and Tennyson. For two hours on end each of them sat smoking his pipe without uttering a word. At last, when Tennyson arose to depart, Carlyle shook him by the hand and said. " Mon, I've had a grand evening."

The only native Irish novel belonging definitely to Ireland's Literary Renaissance which I have come across is " Mrs. Martin's Man," by Mr. St. John Ervine. Mr. Stephens' prose works seem to me to be sheer poetry— the truest, the most elusive, the most beautiful poetry which he has written. His stories, I think, cannot properly be brought under the heading "Irish novels." The making of a novel, even of a " circulationist " novel (if I may borrow an adjective from Mr. Boyd) seems to me to entail a job of work, of sustained and harrassing effort. And, so far as an outsider with necessarily incomplete information at his command may form an opinion, I think that it is just in the capacity for making sustained efforts that the majority of the newer Irish writers fall short. "Mrs. Martin's Man" has an added importance, then—at all events, in the history of the recent literary revival in Ireland—from the fact that it seems to be an almost unique achievement. It is not a first-rate novel as modern novels go, but it is much the best novel by a young Irishman which I have read. In spite of many defects of style and composition it remains a sincere and moving piece of work. It contains some fine passages of description, particularly one or two dealing with Belfast which show the influence of Mr. H. G. Wells. And if in some ways it tends to confirm one in a belief in the spiritual advantages for an Irish novelist of going to Paris with a valet, it does at least reveal a forceful personality capable of bringing a large undertaking to a successful conclusion. I have not read any of Mr. Ervine's plays, but what I have read and seen of the work of some of his fellow Abbey playwrights confirms me in my respect for " Mrs. Martin's Man."

I cannot pretend to have more than a nodding acquaintance with contemporary Irish drama, for the output of plays by the younger Irish writers is far too great for a stranger to explore in a few short months. I thought "Maurice Harte," by T. C. Murray, and "Birthright," by the same hand, read finely, and could imagine that they would be impressive on the stage. In London, about six years ago I remember listening enthralled while Conal O'Riordan read his one-act play "The Piper" in a certain flat in Holland Park Avenue. I have achieved portions of "The Dreamers," by Lennox Robinson which I picked up in a friend's drawingroom in Dublin, and found difficult to tackle. The love scenes between Emmet and Sarah Curran in this play seemed almost ludicrously wooden, though they may be all right on the stage. (I doubt it.) "The Cross Roads" by this author I found more readable, but the comedy "The White-headed Boy," which was given at the Abbey in December, 1916, impressed me as being tedious and ill-constructed, and scarcely redeemed even by the beautiful art of Miss Maire O'Neill. The curtain-raiser preceding the play—it was called, I think, "The Counter-charm," and was by Mr. Bernard Duffy—was just the kind of thing which a clever curate might write for an English parish-entertainment without ever suspecting that he was assisting in a "movement." Other recent Irish plays which I have read or witnessed are "The Country

Dressmaker," by George Fitzmaurice, which left me cold; an extremely capable and efficient (but "un-literary") farce called "The Eloquent Dempsey," by William Boyle; and a one-act symbolist fantasy, by Edward Martyn, called "Romulus and Remus," which was so agonising that I fled from the Hardwicke Street Theatre to the nearest Picture Palace, as fast as the tram-car could carry me. On the whole, I must confess that the suspicion I had already formed in London about "art" plays has been confirmed in Dublin, viz., that to write an "art" play requires in the author just about a twentieth part of the mental equipment, the power of characterisation and presentment and knowledge of the theatre which are needed for the production of one of those contemptible "commercial" plays which bring their authors no kudos but a great deal of money. The name of Mr. W. S. Maugham is one which all interior critics with a devotion to Art, with a big A, no doubt regard with pious horror. I can only state it as my honest belief that there is more truth and wisdom, more talent, and infinitely more literary value in Mr. Maugham's "Caroline" than in half the "artistic" plays which I have come across in Dublin or in London, put together. This is no doubt a heresy: but I must confess that I have no liking for "art" Art: it is too easy. And as long as I live I do not think I shall ever succeed in believing that a bad poetic play about peasants is necessarily more artistic (loathed word) than a clever, well-knit comedy about men and women who move in a more complex state of society. I admire Synge's plays immensely, because he seems to me to have been a very great artist; and I admire Mr. Yeats poems still more, because he also strikes me as being a great artist, and a genius as well. But for the life of me I can discover nothing much either to like or dislike in Irish peasant idiom or in the poetic idiom of the Celtic twilight—by themselves. To me, everything lies in the handling of this material. When Synge or Mr. Yeats handle it, the result is simply astonishingly beautiful. And when very earnest but ill-equipped imitators try to handle it, just because Synge and Mr. Yeats have done so, the results seem to me to be only too often horrid in the extreme.

IV.

OF the making of books about Ireland there appears to be no end. Native men of letters do it repeatedly; it is become a habit; and most strangers (like myself) catch the infection and commit at least one volume. It is impossible to be in Dublin for more than a week without beginning to form opinions about the state of Ireland, or the future of Ireland, or the future of Anglo-Irish relations, or the meaning of the Sinn Fein Rebellion. All Irishmen naturally have their opinions cut and dried on these points, and year after year they discuss them with other Irishmen who have other opinions. And if they don't find a sufficiently large or attentive audience in one another's houses, it is only natural that they should commit their opinions to paper and ensure some attention that way. And in addition to the Irishmen with opinions there is a large and much more hopeful class of Irishmen who have not only opinions, but ideals and faith. The greatest of these is undoubtedly A. E.; but among them must also be numbered the authors of the volumes in the " Irishmen of To-Day " series. Mr. Russell's volumes of essays, however, certainly out-soar all the other books about modern Ireland which I have read or looked at, and, to my mind at all events, his real greatness seems more definitely displayed in them than in either his poetry or his painting. The work which he has done and is doing for the national welfare of Ireland will surely form an inspiring chapter in the Irish histories of the future. He is one of those who are helping to build the Irish State on sure foundations; and his recently

LITERATURE IN DUBLIN 235

published volume "The National Being: Some Thoughts towards an Irish Polity," must have turned many Irishmen's minds away from political controversy towards things which matter more profoundly. There is one suggestion which Mr. Russell has mooted in this book, however, with which many English people (all of whom are, to some extent, in a position to judge) will find it hard to sympathise and impossible to agree. Mr. Russell finds much to admire in the military discipline of conscript armies, and finds nothing odious in the principle of conscription, as such, but thinks the principle of compulsion could be applied to better uses, such, for example, as "the building up of a beautiful civilisation." "While other nations take part of the life of young men for instruction in war, why should not the State of Ireland, more nobly inspiring, ask of its young men that they should give equally of their lives to the State, not for the destruction of life, but for the conservation of life?" "Think," he says, "what an industrial army of 50,000 young men could do for Ireland, building art galleries, sanatoria, public halls, libraries, making roads, recreation grounds, reclaiming waste land, &c. . . ." Such theorising may be all very well for an Irishman who only sees conscription as a more or less distant possibility and therefore knows it not for what it is. I cannot help feeling that public libraries built by slave labour, though they might be more swiftly propagated even than those of Mr. Andrew Carnegie, would be blighted from their birth. Why should not the State of Ireland, instead of introducing a foul and reactionary principle into the national life, administer its public funds with honesty and efficiency? Why should it not, more nobly inspiring, spend the taxpayers' money not on the multiplication of jobs and "money offices," but on the useful and necessary public works which Mr. Russell mentions? I must confess I cannot understand how Mr. Russell can link his splendid conceptions of national service with such an abomination as national slavery. No doubt Mr. Russell has already imagined himself as a young man of the future called on to leave his life's work, the work which he does best, to devote himself for three years or so, together with some tens of thousands of other labourers, to the interesting task of reclaiming waste ground. I am ready to believe that Mr. Russell is great enough, is sincere enough to be able to contemplate such a fate with equanimity. He would not prescribe for others anything to which he was not himself prepared to submit. But, passing over the loss to the community which such a waste of A. E.'s gifts would bring about, let us consider the case of John Smith. John Smith is, let us say, a young musician, absorbed in his art, very clear as to his vocation, a little appalled perhaps—like every artist—at the amount there is to learn and at the shortness of our days. Mr. Russell's conscription machine absorbs John Smith during the most important years of his musical life, and tells him he must ruin his hands in order to help build a public library. An excellent, law-abiding citizen will thus—if he have a little more spirit than a rabbit—be turned against his will into an anarchist, a rebel, or a passive resister. Conscription, whether industrial, idealistic, or merely military, is nothing more or less than legal machinery devised for turning out conscripts. The individual is dropped in at one end of the machine, his personality is ground out of him, and at the other he emerges one of a type, stamped and numbered. Now the trouble is that there are a certain number of people who are *born* belonging to the required type. There are many who are born soldiers. Several millions of them volunteered in the first eighteen months of the present war, and magnificent soldiers they have made. Similarly there are men who are born labourers, born reclaimers of waste land, born builders of art galleries. All these people excel at the different tasks for which they are naturally fitted. Where conscription comes in is obvious. Its business is to perform the unnatural and revolting operation of changing one type into another, crushing human personality in the process. But conscription has the strength and the weakness of all machines; its works are intricate, and if too many stones and other hard substances get entangled in them the machine runs badly, perhaps stops altogether. Can one doubt that if enough Irish backbone and grit—the things which make for greatness in a nation—were to tumble into Mr. Russell's conscription-machine it would explode? Surely it would be of more value to Ireland if her public works were undertaken by a capable Government which paid its workmen fair wages (thus setting a much-needed example to private employers) than if the system of State interference with individual liberty, which Mr. Russell extols, were adopted. I know nothing whatever of the Irish people, and Mr. Russell knows perhaps more about them than any other living Irishman. All the same, I find it difficult to believe that the Irish are by temperament human sheep. In the National Portrait Gallery in Leinster Lawn, where I have spent many hours, I have been struck again and again by the untamed individuality, the oddity, the character in the faces gazing at one from its walls. What original people they are, how splendidly themselves! Is it really the descendants of these people by whose forced labour Mr. Russell proposes to take the bread out of the mouths of Irish bricklayers and artisans? One cannot but feel that the motto of an ancient Scottish house would be subscribed to by all of them, would be subscribed to by all the Irishmen whom one meets in Dublin to-day. The motto is: " Led, not driven."

CHAPTER XI.

The Theatre in Dublin.

My first experience of theatre-going in Dublin was at the Tivoli, a little house on the quays almost opposite the Custom House, with a pleasant "1840" air about it. The place was homely and unpretentious, the programme was mildly amusing, and the audience, mostly very poor people, were good-natured, and beyond a tendency to indulge in occasional cat-calls, fairly appreciative. It was rather astonishing to see what they would put up with. One of the turns was a conjuror, a Jew-boy with a Cockney accent—very nervous, and at the same time very pert—who poured out a flood of stale patter while he drew eggs out of a pot hat, removed fowls from a kettle, and laying a red handkerchief over an empty tumbler removed the handkerchief and displayed the tumbler full of water. The audience bore with him with patience and when, as the grand finale to his performance, he fired a pistol and caused a huge green flag with the harp of Erin on it to flutter down across the stage, he created a positive "fu-ror." The cheering went on interminably, while the Jew-boy, "proud," no doubt, "of all the Irish blood in him," stood bowing and smirking in the middle of the stage. I came away from the theatre feeling that Irish audiences must be exceptionally good-natured and easy to please. A few nights later I went to another hall in Dame Street—the Empire—where much the same thing happened. The house was bigger, the programme not so good, but the audience was cheerful and well-behaved, and seemed pleased with the more agonising turns. One of the turns (not an agonising one) was a " deputy," a child of about twelve who was doing male impersonations in place of an aunt who could not appear. The child came on dressed like a miniature George Lashwood, in a big top hat and London clothes, with a silver-knobbed stick in her hand, and a suspicious green silk handkerchief showing under a buttonhole of pink carnations. It was easy to guess what had been going on behind the scenes. Some kind and experienced female relative had given the little débutante her instructions. She was to reserve her green handkerchief till the end of the turn and then she was to use it to get her " rounds." The child simulated a drunken " Johnny " during two or three dismal songs. ("We'll cling together like the i-vee, on the old garden wall," was one of them). And at the end, sure enough, she took out her little green flag and waved it frantically as she disappeared into the wings. Tremendous applause! Triumph of the kindly relative! I can well imagine that there is a popular saying in the world of music-hall artistes that it really doesn't matter a scrap what you do in Dublin so long as you wave a green flag. The converse of this seems, alas, to be that performers of real talent who care too much for their art to stoop to this easy method of ingratiation, have a very poor time of it in Dublin. The more distinguished they are, the more worth listening to, the poorer seems to be their reception. It was not until after I had visited the two lesser houses that I went to the Theatre Royal, which is the best of the Dublin music-halls. The Royal is a large and handsome theatre, which appears to be very well managed. Its programmes are usually as good as those of the average London suburban music-hall and occasionally better. But, after fairly frequent visits, extending over a period of some months, I must confess that I have not only never met with, but never believed possible, such ill-mannered, rowdy and brutally stupid audiences as those it seems to have the misfortune to attract. Perhaps I have always been specially unlucky: I can only say that I have never been to a " second house " there which was not disturbed by unpleasant interruptions. When a French provincial audience rags the performers in a French revue no one need feel unhappy—the ragging merely adds to the general amusement. The performers usually grin at their own rottenness, the fat ladies in tights know quite well they look ridiculous and don't in the least mind being laughed at —in fact it is often difficult to tell which side is doing the most laughing. Even in Italy, notorious for its cruel and indifferent audiences, I do not believe the appearance of anything like real talent on the stage would fail to exact a tribute of reasonable silence. I remember once in Genoa, in the music-hall in that drafty Via XX Settembre, observing how a rowdy and rather brutal crowd of people suddenly put down their drinks and stopped their noisy explosions when a voice worth listening to made itself heard unexpectedly through the smoky atmosphere. My experience in Dublin, however, at all events at the Royal, has been that the greater is the talent of the performer the worse is the behaviour of the audience. I went one evening to hear a justly popular male impersonator, an admirable "comedienne" whose art, in her particular line, is perhaps only surpassed by our incomparable Vesta Tilley. No sooner had the unfortunate star made her appearance (it was her first night) than boos, cat-calls and loud explosions of laughter came from every part of the house, drowning her completely. I have never before in my life witnessed such a disgusting exhibition in any theatre. I hoped at first that the disturbance might have been due to the presence of an unusually large number of drunks at the back of the pit; but subsequent experience of the Royal has confirmed me in the impression that the audiences at the best Dublin music-hall have a positive hatred of anything above the second-rate. Any appearance of personality on the stage, any display of genius or finesse seems to rouse them to a fury of scorn. During the greater part of my stay in Dublin there was an agitation in the Press about "purifying the music-halls." Dublin audiences were urged to hiss violently whenever anything of dubious purity sullied a comedian's lips. A stranger could scarcely avoid the reflection that it would not have been a bad notion if Dublin audiences had started by purifying themselves. A few elementary lessons in common decency (for example, not to shout down a nervous girl who is trying to earn her living, before she has had time to open her mouth) would not come amiss; and these might be followed up by a more advanced course in theatrical manners as understood in civilised countries. After some such preliminary process of education, Dublin people would be in a stronger position to begin educating their entertainers. I write with some feeling on this point because many of the happiest hours of my life have been spent in theatres, and particularly in music-halls, and it is infuriating to me to see a fine artiste treated with disrespect. I have been forced to the belief that for some reason or other the art of the music-hall is a sealed book to Dublin people. They do not understand it, and therefore, with what looks not unlike provincial prejudice, they elect to dislike it. Even among the Dublin intellectuals, who I imagine never go near the Royal, I have sometimes noticed a curious lack of discrimination, and a tendency to abuse well-known performers whom very likely they have never seen. I have often had the impression that among the Dublin " intelligenzia " as far as the stage is concerned the Abbey Theatre alone stands for " Art " —while everything else, including of course the " red-nosed comedian," is dismissed as " commercial." (How different is the attitude of Mr. George Moore on this point can easily be seen by anyone who cares to turn to his " Confessions of a Young Man," and read his appreciations of Bessie Bellwood and Arthur Roberts). In this respect I think the influence of the Abbey has been positively baleful. By causing one rather restricted branch of dramatic art to be put on a pedestal and worshipped, it has bred a false standard of values in regard to all the other branches. I suppose for the past ten years, certainly for the whole of my life as a writer, I have lived more or less in the atmosphere of the "Art" theatre; but the older I grow the more suspicious I am become of certain of its aspects and tendencies. I have always had the greatest admiration for the genius of Synge ever since I saw "The Playboy" at the Court Theatre in Sloane Square during its first English tour. I have seen some of Lady Gregory's plays and thought them charming; and I can well imagine the beauty of Mr. Yeats' poetic dramas played as the Abbey Theatre Company in its best days must have played them. But I cannot for the life of me leave off admiring the great talent of Miss Gertie Millar or the exotic grace of Miss Gabrielle Ray's dancing or the humours of Mr. W. H. Berry or Mr. Coyne, merely because I also find the Abbey players delightful. Yet this is practically what one is asked to do by many people in Dublin. To them dramatic art is the Abbey Theatre and the Abbey Theatre is dramatic art: and that's that. Mouths screw themselves up into a humorous pout of depreciation when any other plays or players are mentioned. Miss Irene Vanbrugh hasn't the faintest conception of acting; no one but stupid Londoners would tolerate Miss Marion Terry for a moment; and who but a fool lacking in true refinement could discover anything amusing in George Robey? But I am afraid the laugh is really against Dublin theatregoers and not against the stars they jeer at. The "encouragement of native talent" is an admirable and desirable thing, but surely the first step towards a judicious encouragement of talent, native or foreign, is the possession of a just standard of values. He would be but a poor "encourager" of Irish talent who had not such a right standard of values inside himself as would enable him to detect talent in a Hottentot if it existed, or even in an Englishman. The world is a wide place and in the domain of the arts every country contributes something distinctively its own, which should be able to give pleasure to appreciative people. But to be exclusively "Nationalist" in æsthetic matters is clearly an absurdity. If the Irish cannot appreciate "cockney comedians" who are good of their kind, simultaneously with having a just admiration of the Abbey Theatre, the loss is theirs. No people love their own particular stars more devotedly than Londoners. All the same, I should doubt if the Abbey Players have ever had a more enthusiastic reception than they had in Sloane Square.

From a cursory glance at the history of the

Dublin stage, one would gather that in the eighteenth and early nineteenth centuries, opinion went to the opposite extreme in regard to the appreciation shown to native actors, from what now obtains. There were many famous actors of Irish birth in that great age. A writer in 1804 gives a long and distinguished list of players, including Mrs. Jordan, Cooke, John Johnston, and Cherry, who formerly played in Dublin, "but are now absentees from our neglect." While they were in Dublin no one troubled to go to hear them, and he speaks of this as "a satire on our national discernment." Another Irish observer deplores the fact that "Mrs. Kemble, Mrs. Billington and Miss O'Neill were but little respected before they got the London stamp," and observes further: "the fact is no arrangement, no exertions, no sacrifices can satisfy the Dublin public taste; neither stars nor stationary actors can please them."

In spite of this, the amount of dramatic talent available for the amusement of Dubliners between 1754 and 1820 (the lifetime of the Crow Street Theatre) seems to have been remarkable, and in this, as in so many other ways, the city, for its size, compared very favourably with London. Nearly all the most famous players on the London stage found it worth while to come to Dublin; and the theatrical connection was probably stronger between the two cities during those years than it has ever been since.

The most distinguished name in the annals of the Dublin stage in the eighteenth century is that of Spranger Barry who was born in Skinner's Row, Dublin, and began life as a silversmith. He made his stage début at the Smock Alley Theatre in 1744, and was subsequently the head of the Covent Garden Theatre, London, where he became the rival in popularity of David Garrick. Of the two it was said that " with the audiences Garrick commanded most applause, but Barry elicited most tears." His rendering of the part of Othello was immensely admired, and considered incomparable. Thomas Davies, writing a few years after his death observed that " of all the actors who have trod the English stage for the last fifty years, Mr. Barry was unquestionably the most pleasing." Various inducements were offered to him to return to Dublin and build a new theatre there; and he finally decided to take this step in 1754. His agent in Dublin took a lease of the music-hall in Crow Street for him; and in order to admit of the erection of a stage as ample as that of Drury Lane, several contiguous lots of ground were acquired at the same time.

The erection and equipment of the new theatre cost Barry more than £22,000, and his tenancy of it was full of disappointments and distresses, while he also had to encounter the strenuous opposition of the existing playhouses in Aungier Street and Smock Alley. His theatre was opened in October, 1758, was much patronised by the Duke of Dorset, the Viceroy of those days, and was at first fairly successful. After being temporarily closed for some months, it was reopened in 1759 as the Theatre Royal. In 1760 Mrs. Abington was the great attraction of the house; but in the same year Barry sustained a severe blow through the defection of Henry Mossop, one of his principal actors, who went as manager to the Smock Alley theatre. In the last seven years of Barry's management at Crow Street we hear a good deal of Robert Aldridge who was said never to have been surpassed in the various excellencies of Irish grotesque dancing. He composed a ballet called the " Irish Lilt " made up of original Irish airs, which was produced at the theatre. The great Charles Macklin acted under Barry's management in 1765 and 1766 with so much success that he chose Dublin for the first production of one of his plays. By 1767 Barry, owing to Mossop's rivalry, had got into serious financial difficulties and was forced to give up the struggle, Mossop taking his place. Three years later, however, there was another change, and Dawson, manager of a playhouse in Capel Street, took over the management. Dawson "presented" Thomas Sheridan, Spranger Barry and his wife, Isaac Sparks (a famous comedian) and Macklin.

In 1776 the management of the theatre again changed hands, when Thomas Ryder of the Smock Alley theatre, took over the Crow Street house and greatly improved it. Barry died in 1777 and was buried in Westminister Abbey. A later manager at Crow Street was Richard Daly. Mrs. Siddons honoured the house by appearing there in 1793. A little earlier (as the result of disapproval of the way in which the theatre was being run) what seems to have been a kind of Dublin stage society was started in the shape of a "private theatre" in Fishamble Street, under the joint management of the Earl of Westmeath and Frederick Edward Jones. Jones seems to have been a resplendent personage corresponding to the English Regency bucks. He was known as "Buck Jones," and is said greatly to have resembled George IV. both in appearance and in his distinguished manners and deportment. He belonged to Daly's in College Green, the most fashionable gambling club in Dublin in those days, and had a fine house ("Clonliffe") in the northern outskirts of Dublin. He became the last of the managers of the Crow Street Theatre, and seems to have been a man of exceptional taste and judgment. He had the theatre lavishly re-decorated and improved, and under his management Madame Catalini appeared at Crow Street in 1807, Edmund Kean in 1815, and in 1816 Miss O'Neill made her first appearance there.

For some reason or other the authorities ordered the closing of the house in 1820, the unhappy Jones receiving no compensation for the large sums he had invested in it. He died in 1834. It is sad to read that owing to the carelessness of its custodians all the contents of the old playhouse—the magnificent decorations, scenery, benches and even the flooring— were gradually stolen away. The scene room which Jones had erected at a cost of £3,000 became a hat manufactory; and other parts of the empty building were used as a dump for rubbish by the people in the neighbourhood.

An interesting account by Sir Jonah Barrington of the theatres in Dublin in the latter half of the eighteenth century, is quoted by Gilbert. "The playhouses in Dublin were then lighted with tallow candles stuck into tin circles, hanging from the middle of the stage; which were every now and then snuffed by some performer, and two soldiers with fixed bayonets always stood like statues on each side on the stage, close to the boxes, to keep the audiences in order. The galleries were very noisy and very droll. The ladies and gentlemen in the boxes always went dressed

THE THEATRE IN DUBLIN 253

out nearly as for Court: the strictest etiquette and decorum were preserved in that circle; whilst the pit, as being full of critics and wise men, was particularly respected, except when the young gentlemen of the University occasionally forced themselves in to avenge some insult, real or imagined, to a member of their body; on which occasions, all the ladies, well-dressed men, and peaceable people generally decamped forthwith, and the young gentlemen as generally proceeded to beat or turn out the residue of the audience, and to break everything that came within their reach.

" The actresses both of tragedy and genteel comedy formerly wore large hoops, and whenever they made a speech walked across the stage and changed sides with the performer who was to speak next, thus veering backwards and forwards like a shuttle-cock during the entire performance. This custom partially prevailed in the Continental theatres till very lately."

It is interesting to read that Dublin was at one time famous for its " singing halls " and " free and easies," of which there used to be a number near the main entrance to the Phœnix Park. The general impression one gets from reading eighteenth century memoirs is that all the arts of the theatre (in spite of the tendency on the part of the audiences to indulge in riots, *à propos de bottes*) were remarkably well appreciated during that epoch, and that probably no city in the British Isles outside London offered such varied forms of entertainment to its inhabitants. Dublin must have been a gay, wealthy, high-spirited town; and the taste and judgment of the Irish gentry of those times was probably displayed in every department of life, and not only in the fine dwelling-houses and public buildings which they have left behind as their memorials.

To come back to the theatre in Dublin as it exists to-day, one sighs in vain for those exponents of " Irish grotesque dancing " like the great Aldridge, and for the Irish singers who made the Dublin singing halls so popular. The modern Dublin music-halls certainly do not represent Dublin in any way; perhaps that is one of the reasons why, though largely attended, the level of appreciation shown by the audiences is so low. Anyone who has had the great privilege of hearing Miss Maire O'Neill sing a traditional Irish ballad in a drawing-room must regret that there is no real Irish music-hall in Dublin where, like another Yvette Guilbert, she might reign supreme. And what has happened to Irish dancing? Where is it to be seen except in country places or in remote and ominous back streets? It would be a tragedy indeed if this divine art, for which Ireland has been famous throughout the centuries, were to die out.

Of "legitimate" theatres in Dublin there are three, or shall we say three and a half. The oldest of them is I believe the Queen's Theatre, recently rebuilt and very pleasantly re-decorated. In this house I have witnessed an excruciatingly funny melodrama, a still more excruciating performance of "Maritana" by a local opera company, and one of the best Christmas pantomimes I have ever seen anywhere. The Gaiety is the usual theatre of its kind which is to be found in every large town : the theatre to which most of the leading companies " on the road " find their way. Every now and then some very good acting of the despised " commercial " variety is to be seen there. The remaining " one and a half " are the little Hardwicke Street theatre (" the half "), and the illustrious Abbey. The theatre in Hardwicke Street is housed in a beautiful old hall of some antiquity and it is quite an adventure to go to it. The performance, alas, on the occasion of my solitary visit, was not even funny : the "Art" microbe in its most noxious form had blighted everything. There remains the Abbey, a hallowed spot for everyone who cares for the " literary " theatre. Although one may find it impossible to hold quite the same opinion about its players and about some of the plays they put on there as seems to be entertained in Dublin intellectual circles, it is nevertheless the only theatre in Dublin of real interest to a visitor. It is really "Irish," and still unique of its kind. Perhaps it is a pity both for the Abbey audiences and for the Abbey players that foreign plays and foreign actors are not occasionally seen on its boards. A policy of protection sometimes has a more deadly influence on art than it can ever have on commerce. One feels at times that a little less nationality and a higher level of technique might possibly be found to go together. I venture this observation because my first experience of the Abbey—I went there with a heart bursting with excitement—was particularly unfortunate. The theatre itself with its black and gold scheme of decoration, its bare cream-coloured walls, fulfilled all my expectations, and to the sensitive nose had a delightful atmosphere of its own. But the performance—it was a first night of "John Bull's Other Island"—was all to pieces, as if no attempt whatever had been made at stage management. The actors and actresses were absurdly dressed, and had not even learnt their lines. Nora Reilly looked like a rather kittenish hoyden of nineteen, so that her first flirtations with Larry Doyle must have taken place when she was in the cradle. As for the talent displayed by some of the men—Mr. Kerrigan and Mr. O'Donovan for example—

THE THEATRE IN DUBLIN

nothing could obscure it. Anyone could see that Mr. Kerrigan and two or three of his colleagues were fine actors: yet one could not but feel that a few years of the salutary discipline of the despised " commercial theatre " might make them into great actors. There was something vaguely amateurish about that evening at the Abbey; the performance as a whole, though excellent at moments, was ragged. In this respect it compared to my mind very unfavourably with some of the productions of the London Stage Society, where the advantages of the training supplied by the " commercial theatre " are manifest, and the level of Art (with a large A please) is certainly as high. However, it is ungrateful for a stranger to carp at the Abbey. It is a real theatre of ideas; and having already brought to light at least one genius and much remarkable talent, there is always the chance that it will do so again. I know I would sit through any bad play that ever was written if only Miss Maire O'Neill were acting in it. Sooner or later she will inspire some young playwright to do something worthy of her art, of her extraordinary gift of charm; and then the glories of the Abbey will revive. Meanwhile, simply to hear certain tones in Miss O'Neill's voice (they send little cold electric shocks down your spine) is in itself enough to make the pilgrimage to Dublin worth while.

CHAPTER XII.

Farewell!

On the evening before my return to London I sat looking down from my tall window in North Dublin, over the grey city which I had learnt to love almost as much as my own home, thinking over all that had happened to me during my long visit. In the direction of Sackville Street, Nelson's stone effigy rose from among the roofs and indicated the proximity of the chief rebel stronghold. As I looked at it through the gathering mists I felt, rightly or wrongly, that I did not share that complete inability to understand the Rebels' point of view to which a very sympathetic writer in *The Times Literary Supplement* has confessed, in a review of the poems of Thomas MacDonagh. To me their point of view seemed to have a startling, almost naïf simplicity. Their acts seemed to have been prompted from the heart! But do not our hearts sometimes speak the truth to us more clearly than our minds? Which of us really believes in the blindnes of love? Inspiration, moreover, is not only the prerogative of poets and of painters. It does not disdain the simple, nor did it scorn the fishermen by the Lake of Galilee. Through all the fog of talk, through the stinking darkness of professional politics there pierced the lightning flash of their sincerity. The leaders may have been foolish men, or men of only moderate attainments (the Twelve Apostles, too, with the exception of St. Paul, seem scarcely to have been thought much of in the best circles), but at least they were good men, honest according to their lights, most truly self-forgetting. And in the world of corruption in which we live, does not honesty—not that nominal honesty beloved of the commercial mind, that mere refraining from picking and stealing because it doesn't pay, but true honesty of thought and intention—does not honesty stand out now more than ever as the greatest and the rarest of the virtues?

The thought of political honesty in Dublin to-day brings us by a perfectly natural transition to a consideration of the position occupied by Mr. George Russell. He alone perhaps of Irish public men seems to be genuinely *au-dessus de la bataille*. Goodness and honesty as candid as the daylight radiate from him, and the stench of politics does not cling to his garments. Whilst loving Ireland with a passionate idealism, he is nevertheless content to spend his days in hard and most practical work to bring about her good. As his great kindness is as proverbial as his wisdom it is small wonder indeed that the younger generation of Dublin intellectuals look up to him as to a father while the older generation, in any crisis, turn at once to him for inspiration.

The evening shadows were falling now, and the distant hills became a line of frowning black, mysterious and brooding. Soon the lights began to shine out here and there—capriciously, for Dublin is only lighted in patches. The dome of the Custom House, surmounted by its effigy of Commerce, was outlined sharply against the pale sky, but it was too misty to see the sea. I wonder if there was ever a city in the world more haunting in its charm, more touching, more difficult to say farewell to? "There is something about Dublin," people say; and then they stop, not knowing how to continue, for they cannot put into words what they feel, and, to be sure, I can't either. It is miserable and wildly gay; always talkative, sometimes cynical, sometimes idealistic; uncomfortably honest, indecently corrupt; ineffective and yet affecting everyone. And are the inhabitants of any other city so contradictory as the Dublin people? I doubt it. They are sometimes said in England to be fickle, superficial, cold-hearted, untrustworthy and treacherous in friendship, charming to strangers and quarrelsome among themselves. I can only say that I have not found them like this. So far as my experience has shown me, their most noticeable characteristic is the fact that far more than English people they have (except only in matters relating to the Arts) a sense of true values. They have not adopted wealth as their standard, and as they are relentless realists in thought they are singularly free from almost every kind of false sentiment. The ordinary materialistic outlook of the wealthy Englishman is rarely encountered; and I do not think I have ever met a really ill-bred Irishman or Irishwoman of any class. They have often in social matters a refreshing frankness. When they dislike you their rudeness is occasionally unparalleled; but it is never clumsy. Like all naturally well-mannered people they are rarely rude by accident. As a rule I believe they are kind, generous and hospitable to a fault, and their kindness—like their rudeness—is almost always combined with that quick comprehension of other people's feelings which perhaps forms the basis of all good manners. My landlady—a treasure discovered after many previous misadventures, and one of the kindest people I ever met or heard of—is, I think, a typical example of a Protestant Dubliner from the North. She has very bright grey eyes, a sharp thin nose, and thin humorous lips. Her passion for cleanliness is almost painful. She bustles about the big house like a whirlwind, scowling ferociously, ready to give any of us a " good, sound talking to," from the old gentleman on the top floor who on occasions comes home unsteadily on Saturday nights, to myself who am prone to burn the gas till two and to breakfast (alas) at ten. My habits have improved unaccountably since she took me in hand; I quail before that clear grey eye. On one occasion, when the coal man (disregarding her explicit instructions) dirtied the wall paper in my room she gave him such a slap as he is not likely to forget. But to enumerate the kindnesses which this dear woman does on the sly (frowning angrily all the time so that no one's feelings shall be hurt) would require a whole volume. It is enough to say that no one can be in trouble in her house whom she does not help, no one hungry whom she does not surreptitiously feed. She cultivates her bark and her angry scowl as a kind of protection for her warm heart; but it deceives nobody. It certainly does not deceive Nigger, the black cat, who knows perfectly well that the slap he will get for his dissipated habits will be followed by a larger bowl of milk than usual; nor the canaries in the cage in her room, who sing more sweetly than ever when she levels a glance of mock indignation at them, preparatory to giving them their food. And on Sundays, when the work is not quite so strenuous, I love to watch her setting out across the square to church, carefully dressed in her decent black clothes and pretty hat. I often wish my chances of going to Heaven were a hundredth part as good as hers! The only flaw I have discovered in an otherwise perfect character, is her choice of newspapers: she brings up portions of a really wicked sheet to lay my fire with every morning.

Alas, in Dublin, you cannot long escape politics—they are part of the very air you breathe. Now that my stay there has come to an end after several months, I feel far less inclined to hazard political opinions or to form theories than I did when I had been in Dublin a week. Many Irishmen have assured me that politics are the curse of Ireland: I can well believe it. The "condition of Ireland," wherever one goes in Dublin at any rate, is the staple subject of conversation. No doubt it has been the staple subject for centuries. The Irish intellectual seems, indeed, only to be able to escape from brooding on "the state of Ireland" by becoming a voluntary exile. In Dublin he might wish to spend his life meditating on the beauties of the Differential Calculus, or studying the habits of the beetle, that curious insect—but Ireland won't let him. He is like a claimant to some great fortune which is in dispute; he cannot escape from that legacy of hope which every Irishman inherits. He must attend political meetings, talk politics, talk "constructively"; he must assist in the election of Members of Parliament; he must read the Parliamentary reports in *The Times.* All these things he must do with a kind of frenzy of personal interest, and always something is just on the point of happening—and never happens. Usually, when his exasperation is at bursting point he gets a Government job, becomes a cynic, plays a little golf. His son begins it all again.

The most terrible thing, to a stranger, about politics in Dublin is the enormous number of small and antagonistic political parties, which, instead of getting on with the piece, seem to spend their energies in tearing one another to bits in a way which reminds one of Swedenberg's Vision of Hell. And one would gather that no country was ever reviled, despised and loathed as Ireland is by certain Irishmen who live in Dublin. One is often reminded of some eminent person's observation to the effect that "Ireland has bred more heroes and more traitors than any other nation in the world of the same size."

As to the "future relations between Eng-

FAREWELL! 265

land and Ireland," that undying topic, I can only express an opinion now with the utmost diffidence. I cannot help feeling, however, that if the people of both countries could only scrap their politicians and really get to know one another they would be the warmest friends. The quickest way to the complete re-union of Ireland with the Empire seems to be through an exceptionally generous and comprehensive measure of Home Rule. I cannot imagine any appeal to the generosity of the Irish people being made in vain: the way to arouse the generous emotions of others is, assuredly, to be generous oneself. I do not believe that the England which the average Irishman sees bears any relation whatever to the true England. I shall never believe, in spite of recent history, that my country is really militarist at heart. There is, however, a certain type of narrow-minded Englishman, kept exclusively for export purposes, who goes about the world like a misguided fanatic, dropping the dead weight of the white man's burden on the already bowed necks of those unfortunate "backward" races who are too weak to protest. This type of Englishman has for centuries made the mistake of dumping himself and his burdens on to Ireland. Ireland, however, though poor in cash is rich in spirit. There has been trouble, and there always will be trouble until the export to Ireland of British Junkers is once and for all prohibited. When that happens, I see no reason why the friendship between England and Ireland, a friendship based on mutual understanding, should not ripen apace. Both countries will have much to gain by it, but of the two I think England will gain more. The Irish possess essential qualities which the English lack. They are to my mind the salt of the British peoples, the invaluable leaven without which the Anglo-Saxon would grow ever more lumpy.

In Sackville Street one day I noticed a dejected young English farm hand in khaki, looking into the window of a toffee-shop. He had just bought himself some sweets and was wondering if he should buy some more. He had on very heavy boots. As he turned away from the window he trod by accident on the bare toes of a little Dublin paper boy who was offering him a " fin-al Bouff *Ma-il*." The boy withdrew his injured toe with the air of a *grand seigneur*; his dark eyes flashed. He said nothing, but no doubt he thought the more. He lifted his little head, squared his ragged shoulders, and glanced at the soldier. The soldier meanwhile was an object for anyone's compassion. He hadn't meant to tread on the little boy's toes at all. He blushed furiously, then tried to be dignified and failed, pulled some pennies out of his pocket and bought some papers which he did not want and hurried off, inarticulate and clumsy. The honours remained with the barefoot boy with his crushed toe. On the other hand, the poor soldier was not a "brutal khaki cut-throat" in the very least: he was just an awkward, simple fellow with a good heart and rather big feet. I relate this incident for whatever it may be worth, without attempting to point a moral.

Whilst the conduct of the British in Ireland throughout the centuries seems to justify most of the bitter comments which the Irish have made upon it, it can scarcely be contended that the behaviour of the Irish has been perfect. On the other hand, their provocations have been many, and it is absurd to expect a whole high-spirited nation to imitate the virtues of the patient Griselda. We all know how "the woman with a grievance," how the virtuous wife who has been disgracefully treated by a brutal husband, tends to deteriorate morally and mentally as the result of brooding over her sufferings. The Dark Rosaleen, who has suffered so much, seems a little to resemble her. She is always on the point of getting her divorce from the rich, avaricious, stupid husband foisted on her by that wickedest of *mariages de convenance*, the Act of Union. Alas, those who support her in her just cause, have never been able to agree among themselves as to the right line of action to pursue. Some think a Judicial Separation combined with a substantial cash indemnity would be the best thing for the lady. Others, stern moralists, hold the view that—particularly at a time when the rich husband's enemies are attacking him by land and sea—a decent woman should ask only for restitution of conjugal rights. At such a moment, they say, a wife's place should be by her husband's side, the past should be blotted out, all should be forgiven and forgotten. To this the more ardent and honest of the Dark Rosaleen's defenders reply, with indignation, that the marriage was no marriage but a legalised abomination, engineered by treachery. It should be annulled—"no half measures," they cry. The rich husband took advantage of the lady at the moment of her weakness. What could be more just than that the lady's claims should be pressed more vigorously than ever at the moment when the husband is himself embarrassed? The dissensions become furious; the two main schools of thought are absolutely irreconcilable. Meanwhile the only people on the lady's side who keep calm, who retain their air of detachment and their presence of mind, are the solicitors and counsel who have been entrusted with the task of representing her in court. These naturally preserve an even flow of affability, and as the "restitution" party are in a minority, they are prodigal of promises to the ardent ones. But they advise moderation, tact—above all things moderation. And so the interminable case drags on: *Jarndyce* v. *Jarndyce* was as nothing compared with it. Now the jury squabble and have to be dismissed; now the judges cannot agree, and the case is remanded for another few years; now the King's Proctor intervenes with a counter-charge against the appellant's virtue. Meanwhile, the lawyers continue to argue, and to some of the hot-headed it seems as if they intend to allow the case to drag on for ever. Of course, at intervals they try to pacify the poor lady and her more generous supporters with soothing words and facile assurances. "We've got *some* of the judges on our side now," they whisper. "We are certain to get a favourable decision *next* year, if you keep quite quiet and leave it all to us." And they advise good behaviour, courtesy to the other side, and so on. "Above all things," they say, "don't call the old gentleman rude names. It will only put his back up!" And so the lawyers go on talking and proposing bargains and settlements; the gombeen men continue to flourish; and next year comes and nothing happens; and the Dark Rosaleen grows ever more haggard and weary with anxiety. Then at last the young men who love her dearly and who never could understand the Law, nor see any meaning in all the bosh the lawyers talk (seeing only that nothing comes of it, and that the face of their beloved is growing ever more deeply seamed with sorrow), can bear the delays and the suspense no longer, and a sudden madness overtakes them. With bombs and rifles in their hands they march to the doors of the Great Court in which so many millions of words have been uttered and so little accomplished. They create, this little band, a tremendous disturbance with their bombs and their explosions; they startle all the Judges out of their seven senses; they kill, alas, a few of the loyal servants of the Court; and they are killed themselves. But they are glad to die. They were tired of all the writing and all the talking. They wanted to *do* something.

When the commotion calms down, and the lady's younger and too ardent supporters have all been executed and imprisoned the Court continues its deliberations. It continues them still; but it seems to me that things are not the same. The Rebels, pathetic and hopeless as their outbreak was, have achieved something. The Judges are nervous and jangled, a little doubtful of their omniscience. The explosion of the bombs was uncomfortably near their own noses. Moreover, the disturbance has called the attention of the whole world to the dilatoriness and incompetence with which the Irish case has been conducted. The Court, and all the counsel engaged on both sides are suspect. On the rich husband's side the attention of many of his relatives (particularly of his grandsons and great-nephews) has for the first time been attracted to his treatment of his unhappy wife. They consider it an abomination, and will no longer support him in his meanness. And on the lady's side, the outburst of the young men has brought about a still more widespread distrust of the lawyers who, advancing always to the struggle with their drawn salaries in their hands, have nothing but the extraction of a certain amount of alimony in the form of Land Acts (perilously like bribes) to show for their endeavours. Yes: on the side of the Dark Rosaleen, the hearts of many of her supporters go out now to the fools who had no salary at all, but who, nevertheless, in a frenzy of generous impatience, laid down their lives.

THE END.

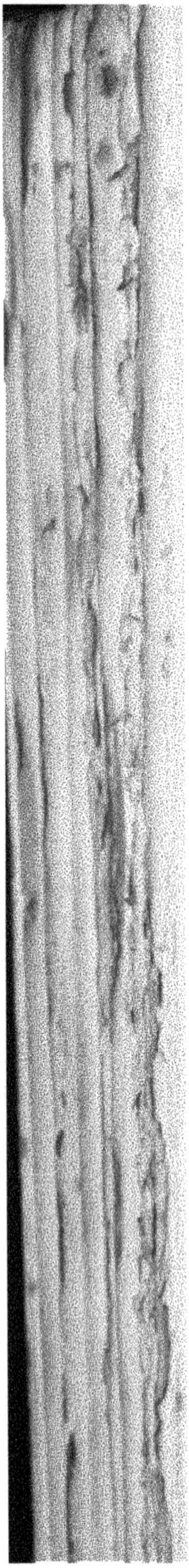

The following Books will be published early in 1917:—

Novels.

CHANGING WINDS. A New Novel, by St. John G. Ervine. Author of "Mrs. Martin's Man," Etc. 6s. net.

The story, which is dedicated to the memory of the late Rupert Brooke, describes the lives of four young men of exceptional promise, and shows how the war destroys the harvest of their lives. The sentence, "Old men make the wars, but they leave young men to pay the price of them," adequately summarises the story, the scene of which shifts from Ulster to Devonshire, from Devonshire to Dublin, from Dublin to London, and then back again to Dublin, where it ends in the Irish Rebellion. There are a variety of interests: love, literary, dramatic, woven into the main strand of the story, which is the longest and most ambitious book yet written by Mr. Ervine, and more than sustains his reputation as one of the wisest and most brilliant of younger novelists.

CHILDREN OF EARTH. A Novel by Darrell Figgis. Author of "Jacob Elthorn," Etc.

Mr. Darrell Figgis' consistent range of work, that has always maintained a high quality in ideals and execution, has won him well into the forefront of modern writers in the English language.

In *The Children of Earth* we have a book that ranks the writer high among his own countrymen as well as among the makers of modern literature. Never, we venture to claim, has the life of the West of Ireland been more intimately handled, for the author lives among the people of the West in a close intimacy that we very much doubt if any other man has won; he has laboured with them, fought land wars with them, and is a son in every house, and it is plain to see from his book that he loves and honours them with a clean and manly affection, free from all sentimentality, as a people who, as he says, possesses an " aristocracy based not on a social cult, but on a native instinct in mind and manners." Mr. Figgis' story is a strong and moving tale, thrown significantly in a scene where Earth rules majestically among her children. The tale is a forcible one, and is a very significant book by a very significant writer.

A YOUNG MAN FROM THE SOUTH

By Lennox Robinson. 3/6 net.

A first novel by the well-known Abbey Theatre Playwright. The hero is a young man of Protestant and Unionist extraction who, coming to Dublin, gradually falls under the fascination of the Gaelic Revival in literature and politics. The book combines the gentle irony of the philosopher with the delicate failing of an Irishman for Nationalist ideals and idealists. There is great intensity in the character study of the central figure in the book, over whom broods always the shadow of a mysterious end. The scene is laid in the Dublin of pre-war days. The book is full of charm and originality, and contains many admirable pen pictures of contemporary life in Dublin.

DUBLIN: EXPLORATIONS AND REFLECTIONS

By An Englishman. 5/- net.

In this volume the author (a well-known English novelist and writer of travel books, who spent some months in Dublin in the summer of 1916) describes his experiences and his impressions of the Irish capital. The author writes of Dublin as he would write of any other foreign capital, that is to say, purely as an outside observer. He is sometimes critical, sometimes enthusiastic; always frank. He gives an interesting account of what he conceives to be the average Englishman's views about Ireland; retails various comments made to him about the Rebellion; writes of the outward appearance of Dublin, its poverty and charm and the beauty of its Georgian houses. Chapters are devoted to the Dublin pictures, and to Dublin literary celebrities and their works. He recalls literary evenings in Dublin, and contrasts them with those of London. He discourses the various aspects of Dublin life which he has observed; and comes to the conclusion that Dublin is one of the last remaining strongholds of liberty. He writes of the frugality of Irish social life, of the wit of Dublin's poor children, of Dublin pawnshops, Dublin drink and Dublin theatres; of Irish passion and intuitiveness; of the future relations between Great Britain and Ireland.

'The book, which is written with great verve, will be accounted one of the most original contributions to the study of Irish life which has appeared in many years.

PADRAIC PEARSE.
Finely printed from hand-set type. Demy 8vo. 7s. 6d. net each volume. The First Vol. contains Plays, Stories and Poems.

A volume containing the original Irish text will follow shortly, and volumes of other prose writings will be announced later.

Padraic Pearse, a leader of the Insurrection in Dublin, 1916, is well known as a distinguished writer in Gaelic, in which language most of his work first appeared. Shortly before the rising he had himself written English versions of his plays and poems, and Mr. Joseph Campbell has now translated the stories, The publishers feel confident that these writings will take a very high and permanent place in Anglo-Irish Literature, and, as well as the intrinsic merits of the work, this book will have the twofold interest of discovering to the reader of English the quality of the work now being written in Gaelic, and of revealing the personality, thoughts and ideals of one of the leaders of the Insurrection.

The first play in the volume, entitled *The Singer*, deals with a rising in the West of Ireland, culminating in The Singer, a wandering poet, whose songs and poems have incited the people to rise, leaving a group of his followers in argument, and going out alone to meet his opponents. This note of sacrifice for one's country is struck again and again throughout the works. The other three plays, *The King*, *The Master*, and *Iosagan*, are cast in a form remote from life, yet as intensely significant as Maeterlinck's work, The stories are mostly from two volumes of Gaelic: *The Mother* and *Iosagan*. The author wrote in a poignant and sympathetic way of various aspects and phases of motherhood. His stories of simple little incidents of child-life are told with a passionate tenderness for childhood and show a profound understanding of the child's point of view. The story of *Iosagan*, where Christ comes to an old man in the guise of a little boy, strikes the keynote of the author's attitude to childhood.

The poems have also first appeared for the most part in Gaelic, an a few, including one written just before his death, have been added.

LABOUR IN IRELAND. By JAMES CONNOLLY, with an Introduction by ROBERT LYND. 4s. net. Contains *Labour in Irish History* and *The Reconquest of Ireland*.

James Connolly is described by Mr. Robert Lynd as Ireland's first Socialist martyr: "a simple historical fact that must be admitted even by those who dispute the wisdom of his actions and the righteousness of his ideals." When *Labour in Irish History* was published several years ago, Connolly was a man unknown outside of labour circles; it was, however, recognized on all sides that here was a new and original interpretation of the historical Irish struggle for self-government. The book is an examination of Irish history in the light of modern Socialist theory, and Connolly did not hesitate in course of it to attack many of the popular gods of Nationalist idolatry. It is a history of the militancy of the Irish poor during the last two centuries, and *The Reconquest of Ireland*, which was first published in 1915 as a pamphlet, describes social conditions still prevailing in Ireland—"this," says Mr. Lynd, "is the prose Inferno of Irish Poverty—and ends on a note of hope for the overthrow of the capitalist society, which was, in Connolly's opinion, so utterly alien to the genius of the Gael."

AN IRISH APOLOGIA. Some Thoughts on Anglo-Irish relations and the war. By WARRE B. WELLS. Cloth 2s. net; paper, 1s. net.

"An apologia," says the author, who is an Englishman with Irish affinities, "certainly does not mean an apology; it means rather a defence or exposition." Though the book is chiefly addressed to the English reader, Irishmen should find much matter of interest in the argument which is written in so true a historical spirit and with so little bias. The author's political associations in Ireland have been Unionist, but his *note* in this book is not polemical, but philosophical. It aims at a consideration of Anglo-Irish relations in so far only as they bear on the war, and essays by a dispassionate enquiry to promote a sympathetic understanding of the Irish attitude towards the war.

BALLYGULLION. By LYNN DOYLE, Author of *Mr. Wildridge of the Bank*. Illustrated by WILLIAM CONOR. 5s. net.

Mr. Lynn Doyle stands high among literary humourists of the day. For several generations, as the writer of a special article in *The Daily Chronicle* points out, Ireland had not given us a genuine humourist, if we except G. A. Birmingham, till the advent of Lynn Doyle. On the publication of *Mr. Wildridge of the Bank* admirers hailed an Irish Barrie. Now *Ballygullion*, a collection of stories mostly of Ulster life, appears with illustrations from the work of Mr. Conor, a new Irish illustrator, also from Belfast—a clever and original draughtsman of whom Ulster should be proud. It is not generally known that there is within the Irish literary and artistic revival a flourishing local movement in letters and the arts which has its headquarters in Belfast. But the collaborators to *Ballygullion* express the temperament of the mysterious province of Ulster better than is done by the speeches of politicians and the articles of newspaper correspondents.

ANNOUNCEMENTS *(continued)*.

New Volume in the "Modern Russian Library."
THE PALE HORSE. By ROPSHIN. Translated by Z. VENGEROVA. 3s. 6d. net.

To this story, which is a translation from the Russian by Miss Vengerova, there attaches at this moment a peculiar interest, for the author, who disguises himself under the *nom-de-plume* of Ropshin is a well-known Social Democrat and took part in the revolutionary movement of 1905. The scene is laid in Russia at the time of the internal disorders that followed the Russo-Japanese war, and these provide the author with stirring incidents and with opportunities for deciphering the temperament of his revolutionary compatriots. Yet it contains nothing of the old conventional and romantic type of 'Nihilist Story.' The object is to show the changed spirit of a new generation of revolutionaries, and a vision of a new and regenerated Russia rises above the sad tale of shattered lives and cruel destinies. The book created a sensation when it was published, and passed through several editions. The author's personal experience gave special value to his revelations, and Ropshin is now considered one of the foremost writers of the younger generation. The keynote of the story is given in the quotation at the head of chapter i.: "And behold a Pale Horse: and his name that sat on him was death."

VERDUN and Other Poems. By H. L. DOAK. Cap. 8vo., wrappers, 1s. net.

"Wrought as they are with simple and severe artistry throughout, they cannot fail to interest any tasteful lover of poetry."—*The Scotsman*, 19th February, 1917.

"Every piece in this collection is artistically a gem."—*Dublin Express*, 5th March, 1917.

"Contains nothing that is not highly finished, concise often to the degree of epigram, and dignified. Mr. Doak has a sturdy thought for expression in every couplet, and the expression is wrought into a diction as concise and polished as that of Mr. William Watson"—*Irish Times*, 3rd March, 1917.

"If we needed an inscription to express some thought or record tersely, tastefully, and exactly, we would confidently entrust the task to Mr. Doak. He is always neat, finished and concise."—*The Times*, 1st March, 1917.

Food Production in France in Time of War. By JOSEPH JOHNSTON, M.A. 6d. net.

Supplementary Report to the Trustees of the Albert Kahn Travelling Fellowship.

"He makes the point that in France all the advantages of decentralisation have been obtained without any of its disadvantages. Perhaps, the best description of his paper which we can give in a word or two is to say that he develops that point at length, with the success of the food production measures as the chief illustration."—*Irish Times*, 26th February, 1917.

Recent Publications

THE NATIONAL BEING
Some Thoughts on an Irish Polity.

By Æ. (Uniform with "Imaginations and Reveries," see page 7).   Cr. 8vo. 4/6 net.

"Stands out among the innumerable social books that stream from the presses like a gentle giant among a crowd of clamouring pigmies."—*Times*.

"Breathes a note of confidence, of hope triumphant and undismayed, of spiritual adventure and high courage that only the ears of youth can catch. Æ's message is not to the politicians of to-day, but to the future nation-builders of Ireland."—*Athenæum*.

"This very nobly written book."—*The Observer*.

"Commands respect as an expression of the aspirations of a true friend of Ireland, and an indefatigable worker in the one field in which a constructive and reconciling policy has been carried to a successful issue in that country."—*The Spectator*.

"A great book for Ireland, and for the socialist movement."—*Labour Leader*.

"This book . . . will be hailed by future generations as a landmark in the arid wastes of speculations on Irish problems."—*Northern Whig*.

"In language that never ceases to be eloquent and sincere Æ makes many fascinating suggestions for an Irish polity."—*New Statesman*.

IMAGINATIONS AND REVERIES

By Æ (GEORGE W. RUSSELL). Uniformly bound with the Author's "Collected Poems." Cr. 8vo. Cloth, gilt, 5/- net.

"Æ is generally regarded as an Irish prophet. . . . There are among men who use fiery speech few in these days so much honoured and so little damned. It is not that he is given to speaking soothing and gracious things. He can denounce his fellows like a Jonah when he has a mind to it. His prose especially is, like so much good prophet's prose, only less apt to fly into a passion of denunciation than into a passion of ideals. . . . Few voices so eloquent in the field of social prophecy have been heard since Mazzini's and Ruskin's. . ."—*The Nation*.

REBELLION OF 1916

By WARRE B. WELLS and N. MARLOWE. Demy 8vo, 7/6 net.

The purpose of this volume is to present an account of the Rebellion, considered especially in its relation to the European War, and of Irish events of the last few years, which shall be impartial and accurate, and may serve, it is hoped, as a standard record of this episode in Irish and European history. In their endeavour to present a record of this character the authors possess the advantage of having been eye-witnesses of the main incidents of the Rebellion in Dublin. They hold that the material evidence, documentary and other, is now sufficiently available.

The volume includes chapters describing fully the strategic importance of Ireland, the personalities and careers of the revolutionary leaders, the literary associations of *Sinn Fein*, and the paradoxical character of the Irish political situation both before and after the events of Easter. In the authors' views the so-called *Sinn Fein* rebellion of schoolmasters was a critical episode of the European struggle for world-power.

It contains as appendices the full text of the Report of the Royal Commission on the Rebellion, the military despatches, and Casement's speech from the dock.

" A remarkable book, written in the true historical spirit. The authors do not aim at defending this or that side, but at presenting both sides. They are detached almost to the point of genius. . . . A fine and fascinating record of an appalling tragedy. . . . The book is not likely to be superseded for a long time. We confess we found it so absorbing that we read every word of it at a single sitting."—*The Daily News and Leader*.

" An interesting, a well-informed, and above all, a thoroughly impartial study of the rising and of its origins. . . . The preliminary study of Ireland's strategic position, and of the ideals of *Sinn Fein*, is instructive, especially to those who do not know much of Ireland at first hand."—*The Times Lit. Sup*.

SIX DAYS OF THE IRISH REPUBLIC

By L. G. REDMOND - HOWARD. Cr. 8vo. Coloured Wrapper. 1/- net.

A critical account of the *Sinn Fein* Rebellion. Mr Redmond-Howard was an eye-witness of many of the incidents. He is already well known as a capable and sympathetic writer on Irish affairs.

" A most interesting account of the recent Rebellion—one of the books on the subject which must be read by those who wish to study the various aspects of the Rebellion."—*Daily News and Leader*.

THE INSURRECTION IN DUBLIN
By JAMES STEPHENS. (Author of "The Crock of Gold," "Here are Ladies," etc.) Cr. 8vo, 2/6 net.

On one side Mr. Stephens' book about the Irish Rebellion is an impression of his own feelings and those of the town during the extraordinary events of Easter week. Of these events Mr. Stephens, the Irish poet and novelist, was an eye-witness, mingling freely with the crowd, and his book is a human document—more valuable than any record of events—which helps one perfectly to understand the emotion of the times. Mr. Stephens knows his Dublin, he has insight into Irish character and aspirations, he has followed contemporary Irish politics; but it is always as the imaginative artist that he writes, not as the student of "the Irish question." In drawing "a moral" from the Rebellion and discussing the future relations of the two countries, Mr. Stephens accomplishes a somewhat remarkable feat: he utters not a single platitude of the newspapers. He believes that friendship between Ireland and England is a possibility; but it will not be based on any compromise of the politicians—generosity is required on the one hand, sincerity and manhood on the other. Those who believe that there is no "new" thing to be said about Ireland should read this book.

". . . . This queer, quiet book, written with an almost inhuman detachment, and yet with passionate interest. . . His comments on the whole help one to understand something of the *Sinn Fein* point of view."—*Times Lit. Sup.*

"The author of this vivid little book observes like a poet, not like a dry student of events. He makes no profession of being the sort of onlooker who sees most of the game; but he does see with remarkable clearness what takes place under his own eyes."—*Westminster Gazette.*

"It is Mr. Stephens' great virtue that he does not sentimentalise the insurrection. He is eager to discover the truth. . . . . A fascinating and provoking story."—*The Star.*

"A remarkable book . . . written with the observant sincerity of an artist. The book is important . . . as a book of personal observation. . . . It brings before us the vision of the Dublin streets amid the strange destinies of Easter week, and suggests the rumorous bewilderment, the quickly-changing passions, the horror, and the human aspect of the city with splendid truthfulness of purpose. A book as sane in mood as it is fresh in manner—a book which everyone should read."—*Daily News and Leader.*

GREEN BRANCHES
Poems, by JAMES STEPHENS. F'cap. 4to, handmade paper. This edition limited to 500 numbered copies. 2/6 net.

Royal 8vo, 7/6 net.

I.—Precursors—James Clarence Mangan, Sir Samuel Ferguson.
II.—Sources—The Father of the Revival: Standish O'Grady.
III.—Sources—The Translators: George Sigerson, Douglas Hyde.
IV.—The Transition—William Allingham. The Crystalization of the new spirit. The Irish Literary Societies.
V.—The Revival. Poems and Ballads of Young Ireland. J. Todhunter, Katharine Tynan, T. W. Rolleston, William Larmanie.
VI.—William Butler Yeats: The Poems.
VII.—William Butler Yeats: The Plays.
VIII.—W. B. Yeats: The Prose Writings.
IX.—The Revival of Poetry: Lionel Johnson, Nora Hopper, Moira O'Neill, Ethna Carbery, and others.
X.—The Dublin Mystics: Æ, John Eglinton.
XI.—The Poets of the Younger Generation: Seumas O'Sullivan, Padraic Colum, James Stephens, Joseph Campbell, James H. Cousins, Thomas MacDonagh, and others.
XII.—The Dramatic Movement: First Phase—The Irish Literary Theatre: Edward Martyn and George Moore.
XIII.—The Dramatic Movement—Second Phase.—The Origins of the Irish National Theatre: W. G. Fay's Irish National Dramatic Company. The Initiators of Folk-Drama: J. M. Synge and Padraic Colum.
XIV.—The Dramatic Movement: Third Phase.—Popularity and its results: " Abbey " Plays and Playwrights. The Ulster Literary Theatre: Rutherford Mayne.
XV.—Fiction and Narrative Prose: George Moore, Shan F. Bullock, George A. Birmingham, St. John G. Ervine, Lord Dunsany, James Stephens, Lady Gregory, other Prose Writers, Conclusion.

BIBLIOGRAPHY.

" A history of modern Irish poetry and drama needed to be written, and Mr. Boyd has written it admirably. His should be a very useful book."—*Daily News and Leader.*

" Mr Boyd has rendered Ireland a service by his critical study of contemporary writers."—*Irish Homestead.*

" His sense of justice holds the scales remarkably even and saves from one-sidedness a clear, always informing, and often penetrating piece of literary history."—*Westminster Gazette.*

IRISHMEN OF TO-DAY

A series of Books dealing with the work of notable Irishmen of to-day and the Movements with which they have been associated. 2/6 net, each Volume.

NEW VOLUMES.

Sir Horace Plunkett and his Place in the Irish Nation. By EDWARD E. LYSAGHT.

Mr. Lysaght, who is both a co-operator and an advanced Nationalist, seeks in this book to interpret Sir Horace Plunkett to those of his countrymen who have hitherto mistrusted or misunderstood him. We have no hesitation in saying that he has succeeded in doing this, and at the same time in providing the British and Irish public with a real exposition of thoughtful Nationalism.

"Mr. Lysaght, a practical farmer, and also a poet of considerable merit, writes well. . . . He is more concerned to discuss Irish policy in a serious and informed spirit than to ventilate his own individual opinions."—*The Times Literary Supplement.*

"Mr. Lysaght is an Irishman of parts. He is a poet of country life, an active Nationalist of the modern school, an Irish speaker, an economist, and a practising co-operative agriculturist. His versatility fits him well to write the new volume in Messrs. Maunsel's series of Notable Irishmen of To-day. . . . ."— *Daily News and Leader.*

". . . . Mr. Lysaght's intimate and delicate appreciation of a new Ireland . . . ."—*New Statesman.*

George Moore. By SUSAN L. MITCHELL.

"An intimate and entertaining literary manner."—*The Times.*

"A brilliantly amusing book . . . . a delightful foot-note to his many volumes of confessions."—*Daily News and Leader.*

"Miss Mitchell combines with a real knowledge of Mr. Moore's work and admiration of his art a sane, witty spirit of criticism which keeps the book free both from dulness and mere adulation . . . . an admirable, vivacious, amusing book which no lover of literature should miss."—*The Observer.*

William Butler Yeats. The Poet in Modern Ireland. By J. M. HONE.

" He writes about Yeats with as little partisanship as a critic who may discuss the life and work of Wordsworth long dead and buried, and yet he understands his author, appreciates him, never shows himself unable to see the real meaning of the words he quotes."—*Irish Homestead.*

" His criticisms are flavoured with a humour which occasionally borders on the sardonic."—*The Spectator.*

" Mr. Hone has written a personal book with rare detachment and restraint, and if one can detect a note of irony in some of his pages, it is so deftly introduced as merely to give an added flavour to the comments and criticisms."—*The Northern Whig.*

Sir Edward Carson and the Ulster Movement. By ST. JOHN G. ERVINE.

" . . . Sir Edward is treated to criticism of the frankest kind, and the Ulster Movement is dissected with the intimate knowledge of one that knows Ireland. The author's analysis of his countrymen is a curious blend of admiration and animadversion, and may recall to some Dr. Johnson's remark that the Irish are a fair people, they never speak well of one another. . . ."—*Glasgow Herald.*

" This is a strong and serious indictment which should make people think. Mr. St. John Ervine hits straight from the shoulder. You have no doubts as to his attitude. Sir Edward Carson is humorously set forth not only as a stumbling block in the path of Irish progress, but as a humorous conception of the first order. . . ."—*T.P.'s Weekly.*

Æ (George W. Russell). A Study of a Man and a Nation. By DARRELL FIGGIS.

" . . . Mr. Darrell Figgis gives an eloquent appreciation of the many-sided activities of Mr. George Russell (' Æ '), one of the most interesting and helpful figures in the Ireland of to-day. . . ."—*The Spectator.*

" The aims and inspiration of ' Æ ' are . . . expounded with force and the keenest sympathy. . . ."—*Manchester Guardian.*

" . . . As a psychological analysis it is a powerful piece of work. Moreover, the many who desire to obtain a summary of Æ's social teaching in some form more compendious than the portly volumes of the *Irish Homestead* will find it brilliantly re-stated, together with a shrewd, critical examination of its theories, in this little book. . . ."—*New Ireland.*

" . . . It creates a pleasant impression of the existence in Ireland of an independent intellectual life. . . ."—*The Leader.*

A Series of Translations of Stories, Novels and Essays, from the best modern Russian Writers.

Two New Volumes. Translated by J. Middleton Murry and S. Koteliansky.

ANTON TCHEKOV AND OTHER ESSAYS
By Leon Shestov. Cr. 8vo, 3/6 net.

Shestov is a writer of small production. But from the time of his second book, "Good in the Teaching of Tolstoi and Nietzsche," which was helped to fame by the famous critic Mihailovsky, he has been highly esteemed by the intellectual elite of Russia. He is essentially a philosopher, yet his own stringent sense of form and his sympathies make of his philosophy an art. He opens a way into the heart of Russian literature which can be followed. His work might even serve as an "Introduction to the true understanding of the Russian Masters."

The work of Shestov, which has been translated, consists of a selection from his various works, chosen to give a foretaste of a writer of quite peculiar subtlety of thought and expression. It contains:—

"Creation from the Void," a brilliant essay upon the inward significance of the work of Tchekov. This is one of the finest examples of contemporary Russian criticism.

"The Gift of Prophecy," a short essay, revealing the same gifts, upon an aspect of Dostoevsky's work—particularly the "Journal of an Author."

"Penultimate Words," a series of reflections upon the ultimate problems of life, and "Philosophy and Knowledge," afford a glimpse into the philosophic tendencies of the most acute minds of modern Russia.

PAGES FROM THE JOURNAL OF AN AUTHOR
By Dostoevsky. Cr. 8vo, 2/6 net.

This book is composed of the two most famous and most typical portions of the *Journal of an Author*.

The story entitled "The Dream of a Queer Fellow" contains the quintessence of Dostoevsky. It is the mature and terrible expression of the conclusion to which the seeking of his life has led him. It is, speaking soberly, one of the great masterpieces of the nineteenth century.

The famous address on Pushkin, with which Dostoevsky stepped at one stride into the position of the uncrowned King of Russia. It is his testament to the Russian nation, his confession of his belief in the Russian soul.

THE RIVER OF LIFE.

By Alexander Kuprin. Translated by J. M. Murry and S. S. Koteliansky. 3/6 net.

The Translator, in his preface, writes, Kuprin is an artist who has found life wide and rich and inexhaustible. He has been fascinated by the reality itself rather than by the problems with which it confronts a differently sensitive mind. Therefore he has not held himself aloof, but plunged into the riotous waters of the River of Life. He has swum with the stream and battled against it as the mood turned in him; and he has emerged with stories of the joy he has found in his own eager acceptance. Thus Kuprin is alive as none of his contemporaries is alive, and his stories are stories told for the delight of the telling and of the tale. They may not be profound with the secrets of the universe; but they are, within their compass, shaped by the perfect art of one to whom the telling of a story of life is an exercise of his whole being in complete harmony with the act of life itself.

THE BET AND OTHER STORIES

By Anton Tchekov. Translated by J. M. Murry and S. S. Koteliansky. 3/6 net.

"The output of English translations of Russian literature continues apace, and 'The Bet' and other stories . . . is a specimen of the work at its best. The translation is very good. It reads like English, yet it maintains the Russian atmosphere. It has none of the stiffness nor the triviality of 'translator's English,' and the prose always fits the matter as live prose should . . . Tchekov is not depressing as our own little realists are depressing, because the triviality and the meanness are not inherent in the people themselves. They are not, like the characters drawn by our own realists, engaged in making a mess of life by their own stupidity or conceit. Some of them are bewildered, wrongheaded, or childish; all of them inspire sympathy, not blame. And it need hardly be pointed out now how exquisite an artist is Tchekov in his elusive 'static' manner. His sense of proportion is so fine, his understanding of each case is so complete, that he can always suggest a great deal more than he tells. He draws you, gently but irresistibly, right into the heart of the matter, and takes you captive with a motion of the finger."—*Times Literary Supplement*.

WITH A DIPLOMA.

By V. I. Nemirovitch-Dantchenko. Translated from the Russian by W. J. Stanton Pyper. 3/6 net.

"Nemirovitch-Dantchenko is a terse, effective raconteur."—*Times Lit. Supplement*.

"'With a Diploma' take us straight to the heart of rural

IRISH ECLOGUES. By Edward E. Lysaght. Quarter Parchment, 3/- net.

"Mr. Lysaght, unlike many poets, not only praises a country life, but lives it and does its hard work. Nor does this practical experience get in his way; his eclogues have a rare and excellent flavour about them, a real smell of the earth, that is satisfying and good. All dwellers in the town will be grateful to Mr. Lysaght for putting them in such close touch with his deep love and knowledge of the country."—*The Observer.*

LOVE OF IRELAND

Selected Poems by Dora Sigerson Shorter. F'cap. 8vo, 2/6 net. A volume of Poems relating to Ireland, selected from the Collected Edition and other volumes.

"Quick with the romantic love of Ireland. . . . These are poems from the heart. 'Love of Ireland' is a book of lyrical and passionate tenderness."—*Daily News and Leader.*

"Among living interpreters of Ireland, Dora Sigerson has won for herself a high place."—*The Graphic.*

"All beautiful, and all individual."—*Daily Express.*

THE MOUNT OF TRANSFIGURATION

A Volume of Poems by Darrel Figgis. 3/6 net.

Author of "Jacob Elthorn," "A Study of Shakespeare," "Queen Tara," &c. Cr. 8vo.

Mr. Figgis has beauty at his command . . . he can raise his voice to a noble salute of life.—*The Standard.*

WILD EARTH and Other Poems

By Padraic Colum. 3/- net.

This volume takes its name from a collection of poems of peasant life published in 1909. While some of those poems are included in the present volume, poems of a different character have been added and the series of peasant poems has been made more complete.

ANNOUNCEMENTS *(continued)*.

THE ROSSES and Other Poems. By Seumas O'Sullivan. This edition limited to 500 copies for sale. Finely printed on handmade paper, 5/- net.

Mr. Boyd, in his recent book, refers to Seumas O'Sullivan's *Poems* as being " one of the finest books of contemporary Irish verse." He goes on to say :—" O'Sullivan's verse has been, for the most part, concerned with the gentle, pensive emotions of the singer who celebrates the soft beauties of twilight. The shadows of the poplars, the reeds and sedges of lonely moorlands sway in a delicate rhythm which his ears have caught. He would ' seek out all frail, immortal things,' the white gleam of ' foam-frail ' hands, the murmuring leaves, the gleam of ' light tresses, delicate, wind-blown,' and of these he makes his song in praise of beauty. He is unexcelled as a painter of soft-toned pictures pervaded by the quiet of evening solitude. The Path, The Sheep and The Herdsman are striking examples of this faculty of evocation, in which the interior harmony of the poet with his surroundings is expressed : and as he watches, happy memories crowd in upon him, but they pass away like the spectacle before him.

"Almost all O'Sullivan's poems are saturated with a wistfulness, springing from the consciousness that our moments of perfect happiness are gone before we can realise them, to return no more except perhaps as the burden of some sad reverie. They are ' delicate snatchings at a beauty which is ever fleeting,' as Æ describes them."

EARTH OF CUALANN. By Joseph Campbell. With Twenty-one Designs by the Author. This edition limited to 500 copies for sale. Finely printed on handmade paper, 5/- net.

The ancient district of Culann belonged, for the most part, to the County of Wicklow, but it spread north and north-west to within a short distance of Dublin. Wild and unspoilt, a country of cairn-crowned hills and deep, watered valleys, it bears even to this day something of the freshness of the heroic dawn. It is out of this country that these songs have sprung. Mr. Boyd, in *Ireland's Literary Renaissance*, devotes nine pages to Mr. Campbell's work. He says : " When he sings of the simple things of Irish life he is unequalled." *Irishry*, he says, contains " a series of pictures whose every stroke catches the eye of imagination. . . . All the beauty, dignity and pathos of Irish country life are preserved."

It is expected that the limited edition of above two books will be exhausted before publication. Lovers of poetry should order now so as to secure copies. Collectors should take the opportunity of obtaining copies at the original price, as the books will probably increase in value after publication.

Cr. 8vo., 4s. net. Contains *The Fiddler's House, The Land, Thomas Muskerry.*

The above three plays are out of print in the original and separate form, and are now printed for the first time in a collected volume.

Mr. Boyd, in his recent book, writes:—"Padraic Colum was the first of the peasant dramatists, in the strict sense of the word; he was, that is to say, the first to dramatise the realities of rural life in Ireland. Where Synge's fantastic intuition divined human prototypes, Colum's realistic insight revealed local peasant types, whose general significance is subordinate to the immediate purpose of the dramatist."

FOX AND GEESE. A Comedy in Three Acts. By SUSAN R. DAY and G. D. CUMMINS. Paper, 1s. net.

"A very amusing play, written in that rich dialect of which Synge and Lady Gregory have made such literary use. This comedy is full of unexpected turns and phrases, and can be read with great enjoyment, because on every page one comes across some notable and original phrase."—*Irish Homestead.*

"The piece is in fact the drollest and most audacious farce that has been seen in Dublin for a long time; and from the point of view of exciting the audience to laughter, its success was complete."—*Evening Herald.*

"'Don't miss it' is the best criticism for *Fox and Geese.* But of more importance than the well-constructed plot, its natural development, and the climax of the concluding line, is the rich wording of the play."—*Irish Times.*

THE LORD MAYOR. A Comedy in Three Acts. By EDWARD MCNULTY. 1s. net. (*Ready shortly.*)

THE HOOK IN THE HARVEST. A Drama in Three Acts. By REV. P. A. DOYLE, O.S.A. Wrappers, 1s. net.

A drama of Irish life about the year 1852.

MAUNSEL AND COMPANY, LTD.
50 LOWER BAGGOT STREET, DUBLIN
40 MUSEUM STREET, LONDON

Lightning Source UK Ltd.
Milton Keynes UK
UKHW041010030119
334850UK00011B/1754/P